LEARNING VALUES LIFELONG
From Inert Ideas to Wholes

D1525691

VIBS

Volume 132

Robert Ginsberg
Founding Editor

Peter A. Redpath
Executive Editor

Associate Editors

a volume in

Philosophy of Education
PHED
George David Miller, Editor

LEARNING VALUES LIFELONG
From Inert Ideas to Wholes

Michael M. Kazanjian

Amsterdam - New York, NY 2002

The paper on which this book is printed meets the requirements of "ISO 9706:1994, Information and documentation - Paper for documents - Requirements for permanence".

ISBN: 90-420-1600-0
Printed in the Netherlands

This book is gratefully dedicated to

the loving memory of
Florence Hayden Towne
"The Second Jane Addams"
Head Resident at Erie Neighborhood House (1926-1951)

and

the loving memory of
Fannie Remmer
Devoted Assistant to Florence Hayden Towne

CONTENTS

EDITORIAL FOREWORD

Life-long learning is now in vogue in many of the institutions of higher learning. How seriously these institutions value life-long learning is another thing entirely because these same institutions created the problem in the first place with curricula designed for resume building and smooth entrance into specific economic niches instead of enrichment of the human soul. Diplomas have become less an indication of achievement, and more like death certificates, indicating when intellectual rigor mortis sets into graduates/victims.

In *Learning Values Lifelong*, Michael Kazanjian offers a new path for life-long learning. Life-long learning can be reanimated, Kazanjian argues, when we view human beings and learning as process. The educational system creates dead, inert minds because of what it stuff students with—inert ideas. Inert ideas, a term Kazanjian borrows from Alfred North Whitehead, fail to engage human beings. They fail to excite or intrigue students. Inert ideas are the cold facts that deaden the quest for intellectual development.

Advocating process learning, Kazanjian describes talks about education as rehumanization and human becomings. By these terms, he means that life-long learning is more than acquiring new job skills. Life-long learning addresses the whole human being instead of just that aspect to be affixed to an economic structure.

Learning Values Lifelong explores pressing concerns in higher education, including distance learning and the information explosion. While it can never replace face-to-face interaction, distance learning can be an effective interactive educational experience. Inert ideas are the result of the information explosion. The pure volume of information overwhelms people, who often lack the skills to simplify and theorize it. The information glut is only going to get worse and life-long learners require a way of assessing it.

"Value means," Kazanjian writes, "that rehumanization or wholeness is evolving as our dignity and nature." Life-long learning is intrinsically related to developing the full spectrum of our humanity. This is not only crucial to the souls of students, but also to the soul of the body-politic, which in our troubled times needs visionaries who can think holistically and recognize global problems require global solutions.

George David Miller
Editor
Philosophy of Education Special Series

ACKNOWLEDGMENTS

My sincere thanks to George David Miller for accepting my present work as part of the Value Inquiry Books Series in Philosophy of Education. He has been as eager as I to get this manuscript into print. Fortunately he has beeen more patient, critical, and far sighted than I in insuring this book's intellectual respectability. I am always grateful to work with an editor who is one step ahead of me.

Rodopi Executive Editor, Robert Ginsberg, consistently finds ways to improve book manuscripts. I have learned more from his counsel than I can put into words. Repeatedly I have posed questions to him requiring, I thought, one word or brief replies. His impeccable judgment has invariably dissected the complexity and broader dimensions of my query. The results have meant insightful conversations in which Robert Ginsberg has taught me so much more about my goals than I thought possible.

I can never adequately thank Managing Editor Eric van Broekhuizen for his expertise in the mechanics of publication. He is unequalled in his professionalism and humanity.

Thanks to my colleagues and friends, Triton College Dean of Liberal Arts, Edmund C. Forst, Jr., and Loyola Professor, Robert H. Lichtenbert for their continuing support and encouragement. I bring them endless problems and questions; they fortunately respond with answers I need but often do not want to hear.

My Chapter on the information explosion has been an especially tricky one. I have learned much from the Doctoral Dissertation of Mark Donald Bowles, concerning this topic. He has graciously reviewed a version of the chapter and offered vital suggestions.

Grace Budrys was kind enough to suggest that her family member living in another State, Paola Lortie, could help me with questions about John Dewey. I have the feeling that Paola Lortie knows as much about John Dewey's writings as did Dewey. I am indebted to Lortie for promptly providing me with material about Dewey, without which my references to him could not have been included. My appreciation to Budrys for acting as intermediary and messenger between Lortie and myself.

Thomas J. Murphy and Leigh Maginnis gave me much insight into the issues of specialization and subspecialization involving chemistry and biology, respectively. I appreciated the time each generously gave to listening to me about my project. The data they gave me were invaluable, The directions in which they pointed became beacons for discovery beyond what I imagined.

Members of the Reference Department of DePaul University Libraries have been magnificent. Margaret Power, Terry Taylor, Susan Clarke, Rosemary Cooper, Robert Acker, Jeffrey Kosokoff, and Kara Malenfant are research geniuses. Time and again they have answered what I felt were unanswerable questions. More than once they helped me by rewording my searches. I have thanked them for their past assistance, to which they have responded that they had forgotten that they helped me. This acknowledgment hopefully shows the world that I have not forgotten their kindnesses. My apologies to all other members of the reference department whose names I have unintentionally omitted, and whose help has been critical.

John Rininger of DePaul University's Interlibrary Loan Department is in a class by himself. If he ever joins the Federal Bureau or Investigation (FBI) as a Special Agent, the Bureau would have one more superior investigator. His tenacity, patience, and ingenuity in researching material for endnotes has been the difference between my having and not having critical references I needed. He has the uncanny ability to find a single name or word written on a page written in print so small that the writing makes fine-print look like large-print.

My thanks to the readers: Susan Arenz, Laurie Melvin, Cynthia M. Simko, Erin Ramsden, and Jack Johnson.

My acknowledgments imply that all the people are so intimately associated with this work that these persons are responsible for the final version you are reading. That view is partially true. Any success resulting from this book is due mainly to the efforts of the persons above. I am the person taking or refusing advice for my final verson. I take full responsibility for all shortcomings in the following pages.

MK
Chicago, 2002

INTRODUCTION

My present book is aimed at scholarly readers in the philosophy of education. I argue that lifelong learning is based on a process philosophy of education. From the perspective of lifelong learning, education occurs throughout life. Process philosophy of education says that learning in an ongoing development that we never complete. Educators in lifelong learning have in common with process philosophers of education the approach that education is a continual, unending development.

The following pages argue that students continue to learn after they graduate and enter the workforce. Workers periodically return to school to think about work. Students do not leave behind their nature as learners upon graduation. Workers are always students. The process philosophy of lifelong learning means the holistic perspective of values. Workers are human beings always learning about their irreducibility to production. Workers are fundamentally evolving, whole, human beings becoming more competent employees. Developing or evolving human beings are becoming increasingly aware of their holistic values as growing persons. Values help human beings to always humanize or make more whole all aspects of work and thought.

Throughout this book I use terms *rehumanization* and *human becomings*. Workers return to school in order to continually humanize work and thought. Humanizing jobs and academe does not occur just once. Students rehumanize work and thought throughout life. The rehumanizing process means students must try to understand work as done by human beings and not just mechanical activity. Students as student-workers or worker-students need to continually understand the holistic view of work as a human activity based on values. Humanizing work and knowledge and eliminating dehumanization is lifelong.

Human beings are always becoming more whole as they rehumanize production and academia. Workers as students are constantly thinking of work and knowledge in terms of holistic, humanizing values of community, continual maturity, and human dignity. Rehumanization involves human beings in process. Lifelong learning means the ongoing, unending process of human becomings increasingly holistic. Wholeness reveals our nature as human becomings continually rehumanizing ourselves and society. Becoming more whole by rehumanizing work and learning expands the view of traditional lifelong learning.

Lifelong learning usually denotes that workers return to school to relearn job skills. I am not opposed to that view. My point is that lifelong learning concerns more than relearning jobs. Ongoing education is the lifelong learning of values and wholeness in all aspects of work and learning.

From the perspective of lifelong learning, workers are always students. As students, all workers periodically return to school to relearn jobs skills. Returning to school must be a human or holistic social process within the context of ethics or values. Returning to school cannot be simply a mechnical process devoid of ethical underpinnings. Schooling ought to always be value-laden or ethics oriented. People are irreducible to the passive performance of work and to the passive listening to lectures.

Alfred North Whitehead protests against "inert ideas" or "dead knowledge."[1] He says that students are alive and never passive receptacles for cold facts. They always seek to grow intellectually, culturally, and physically. His work is an excellent example of the process philosophy of education. He would be an outstanding advocate today for lifelong learning. Alfred North Whitehead would be an outspoken advocate of values and wholeness in lifelong learning.

My present volume concurs that inert ideas must be replaced with process learning. Looking inside varying aspects of academia, I argue that lifelong learning as a process philosophy of education can replace inertness with continual rehumanization in various academic structures.

Chapter One says that learning is lifelong. Education ending with graduation is inert learning. Students learn about work without values. A process philosophy of education replaces inert learning with lifelong education embodied in values and wholes. Jobs which never change are inert careers and must be replaced with the view that professions evolve toward wholeness and deepening of values. Lifelong learning instills students with the values of ongoing education. We rehumanize work as workers periodically return to school to learn new ideas, and relearn fundamental ideas such as the reality of lifelong learning. Human beings relearn their nature as human becomings continually developing toward wholeness.

Chapter Two argues that teacher-student community is lifelong in distance learning. Inert distance learning occurs in traditional public television where professors lecture to city-wide viewing audiences who cannot physically participate in the televised sessions. Lifelong learning replaces inert distance learning with interactive distance learning. Interactive distance learning fosters teacher-student interaction. Interaction manifests a sense of community. The communal context means rehumanizing the technology by using sophisticated equipment constituting an electronic infrastructure facilitating imparting of values. This chapter does not endorse interactive distance learning for all courses or subject-matter. I want only to say that if and when we require distance learning, the technology allows teachers and students to interact through the values of community as much as possible. Teachers and students must always learn their nature as human becomings rehumamizing technology by continually putting technique in the context of community.

Chapter Three concerns the lifelong need for traditional classrooms. Interactive distance learning and Internet may have their place. Lifelong learning teaches the value of the classroom as the primary means of teaching and learning. The classroom should not be replaced by technology. Total replacement of physical classrooms with distance learning and the Internet reduces even interactive distance learning to inert classrooms lacking the value of face-to-face interaction. The classroom's face-to-face interaction must be the primary method or context for the teacher-student relation. We rehumanize teaching and learning by arguing that human becomings need the classroom's holistic, face-to-face context for most education.

Chapter Four considers the values underlying the information explosion. Allowing the information explosion to occur without periodic simplification and reorganization reduces quantities of data and theory to inert quantities of information. Inert quantities of information lack humanizing values of theoretical reorganization of data and special theories. Simplicity is a lifelong value giving ongoing organization to the information explosion. The information explosion needs ongoing structure and simplification. Lifelong learning as a process philosophy of education means we need to always consider the holistic general theory or set of theories underlying and giving meaning to increasing quantities of theory and data. Human becomings rehumanize increasing amounts of information by continually developing data and special theory within the context of generalized theory.

Chapter Five shows that liberal arts gives interdisciplinary and social values to disciplinarity or specialization. Liberal arts must be as lifelong as is specialization. Inert disciplinarity occurs when disciplinarians do not communicate with each other, fail to develop social skills, and refuse a homological approach to general education. Returning to school, workers as students must continually respect those in other disciplines, grow socially as well as intellectually, and seek homological unity among specialities. Lifelong liberal arts helps rehumanize disciplines and show the complex, integrated nature of human beings as human becomings.

Chapter Six goes inside specialized study. Values comprise all disciplines. Every discipline involves lifelong need for intradisciplinary thinking about doing. Alfred North Whitehead would argue that specialized motions and techniques without thinking constitutes inert specialized study or inert intradisciplinarity. Lifelong thinking within specialized study allows students to understand that evolving, holistic human becomings are studying a specialty's motions and techniques. We rehumanize disciplinary motions and procedures by seeking to understand their holistic contexts and direction.

Chapter Seven goes inside general and specialized learning. In each case, theory is as lifelong as data. If we look upon data as something to be memorized without theoretical foundations, we are guilty of inert data. Lifelong attention to theory gives holistic, human context to data.

Chapter Eight concludes my book. I emphasize what happens when our educational system is clogged with inert ideas. The dangers of inert ideas starting in schools and extending to all society, are put forth in a compelling manner. Students studying those inert ideas are like people infected with contagious disease. Students become workers carrying inert ideas into the working world. Those ideas spread to create crises throughout education, work, family, neighborhood, environment, and the world.

These chapters demonstrate that lifelong learning is more than returning to school to relearn jobs. Lifelong learning is fundamentally about values throughout various levels of relearning. Values mean that lifelong learning is a complex structure. Workers return to school for ongoing learning. If and when learning involves technology, community underlies distance learning. The classroom's face-to-face concept is the primary method of teaching. As we teach, continual resimplification or reorganizing of vast quantities of data and theory provides values and humanization to the information explosion. Reorganizing knowledge involves the continual study of liberal arts as basic to specialization. Liberal arts are ongoing wholeness as homologies. Inside specialization, thinking about doing as disciplinary motions gives values to intradisciplinarity. Finally, continual thinking about data provides theoretical structure to information.

Values and the holistic perspective comprise a systematic framework as the humanizing nature of lifelong learning and this book. My chapters are more than a juxtaposition or succession of ideas. Each chapter indicates a value which contains or encampasses other values about which we read in following chapters. Reality is not divided into values and the value-free. We do not add value to the value-free. Value-free existence is impossible.

Value is never external to technical, material, cognitive, quantitative, or other objective aspect of existence. Value means that rehumanization or wholeness is evolving as our dignity and nature. We need to understand that human existence is an ongoing process of learning. That process enables us to put technology, work, information, and other quantitative dimensions of life into a direction for human beings. Lifelong learning helps teach us that we are never done with the efforts to eliminate dehumanization and ignorance. The educational system is society's tool for understanding and tackling the problems of stagnation in work and learning.

A process philosophy of education instills rehumanizing values and wholeness to prevent fragmentation in work and knowledge. Human beings become better enlightened about their holistic, evolving nature as they study more and more of themselves as human becomings striving toward increasing intellectual-physical-affective-and-social wholeness.

Chapter Five orients this book. I present the other chapters as aspects of lifelong learning. The ideas of ongoing education, learning technology and the notion of the classroom, and the information explosion indicate the social and cognitive contexts and values of lifelong learning. The notions of thinking about doing and the theory-data continuum show that disciplines are irreducible to action and data. Chapter Five concerns the liberal arts as foundations of lifelong learning.

Chapter Six pulls together the ideas from the other six chapters and demonstrates their unity as isomorphic or homological values needed throughout life. The liberal arts comprise the basic values giving meaning and roots to work and study. We learn to rehumanize work through lifelong learning, distance learning through interaction, and teaching-learning location through the classroom. We learn to rehumanize the information explosion in terms of simplicity, disciplines through liberal arts, action through thinking, and data through theory.

Lifelong learning is more than returning to school to study for another job. Ongoing education means learning to relearn, to rehumanize ourselves and society, to become a more complete human being, to discern wholeness and value in existence.

Lifelong learning is a process philosophy of understanding work and knowledge as the ongoing revelation of truth. Truth is never static; rehumanization discloses reality everyday as human becomings grow and mature. Truth is not revealed just once. Human becomings reveal truth each time they become more than they have been. Each time we approach life in a holistic way, each time we understand and implement values, we reveal truth and a better society.

One

REHUMANIZING WORK

Learning is lifelong. Education never stops. We are always learning. Education is a dynamic, evolving process continuing throughout life. Life is learning. Students earn their degrees and work until retirement. Some people work after retirement. Learning also occurs after retirement. Lifelong learning means that workers and retirees must periodically return to school to relearn. Human beings are always developing themselves.

Work is part of the study-work continuum. Workers are evolving human beings who need continual learning. Ongoing education humanizes or rehumanizes work by giving meaning, purpose, and direction to productivity and careers. Dynamic human beings work. Dynamic human becomings work. Human beings are irreducible to even the most rewarding jobs. Workers are first and always holistic persons in an evolving context. Values and wholes as lifelong learning reject the inert ideas of reducing people to workers.

1. We Learn to Learn

We must learn to always learn. Working throughout life is wrong when workers never learn beyond their years of formal education. Jobs appear and disappear. Professions that continue will at the very least evolve. Evolution requires relearning. Students cannot be satisfied with only working after graduation. Learning throughout life means that we learn values and wholeness instead of only working. Work within the holistic context of values and wholenes rejects the inert ideas of value-free work and education.

The process philosophy of education in terms of learning throughout life is akin to the sociology of work. Sociologist of work, Fred Davis, points out that work is irreducible to "crass" or dehumanized productivity in the workplace lacking values and a sense of wholeness. He says that the workplace is based upon and expresses "non-instrumental values"[1] between producer and consumer. Those values mean that workers are fundamentally human beings.

From the perspective of lifelong learning, life after graduation is irreducible to the value-free, dehumanized practice of going to work and never returning to school. Life is not devoid of periodic relearning for improved productivity and existence. Lifelong learning is a non-instrumentality giving holistic meaning and value to work. From the perspective of lifelong learning, life is irreducible to work.

Work-without the value of ongoing education is crass and dehumanizing. A job is the instrument with which to earn a living and evolve as a worker and person. More deeply, any job or field of work requires the non- or pre-instrumental value of ongoing learning and rehumanization of work. The pre-instrumentality of ongoing education helps workers see themselves as evolving human beings, or as I put it, human becomings.

Workers are not just doing or using an instrument such as specific knowledge, equipment, and actions when producing goods or rendering a service for a client. Workers are primarily thinkers who think about what they do as careers, and during their workday at the workplace. Students must think about work as well as prepare for jobs by learning technical skills.[2] From the perspective of my present chapter, doing means a career or job field. Learning comes through reflecting upon or thinking about doing or our profession and not just working in that field. Lifelong learning says that a career means doing, and school is the ongoing opportunity to think about careers as doing. Workers must acknowledge a sense of morals, ethics, and community as the pre-instrumental foundation, direction, and context of jobs. Workers are one with the consumer, doing something practical within ethical and socially uplifting constraint. From the perspective of ongoing education in relation to work, traditional education teaches primarily instrumental knowledge and does so once. When students graduate with their degrees, they no longer return for continual learning. Lifelong learning's process philosophy of education teaches students the basic non- or pre-instrumental value or whole: learning that learning is lifelong.

Lifelong learning is as necessary as work. Dean of Humanities and Social Science at Massachusetts Institute of Technology (MIT), John E. Burchard says specialization is here to stay.[3] Henry Winthrop points out that specialization is indispensable.[4] John E. Burchard and Henry Winthrop concur that specialization or work is lifelong. The process philosophy of education says that education is also lifelong. Ongoing learning is here to stay and indispensable as is specialization.

Colleges and universities teaching lifelong learning are imparting the values of motivation. They do not just teach facts or practical techniques. Japanese educator, Reiko Yamada, suggests that we may define lifelong learning as learning that is a lifelong process built upon motivating people to learn continually.[5] Motivation helps students overcome the inert ideas of being passive listeners and unthinking doers.

Traditional learning assumes that we teach students something that they will retain throughout their lives of work. In traditional learning, the educational process is an effort to teach students a static content instead of motivating them to learn throughout life. Lifelong learning embraces the idea that schools must impart the values of motivation to learn continually.

Motivating students takes priority over giving them details and facts. Students who are instilled with the will to learn can learn many things over time by taking the initiative to become educated. Alfred North Whitehead speaks about education as provoking the students' initiative and not just giving them knowledge.[6] Students instilled with the idea of always learning have learned the most valuable lesson in education: we are a learning species. Learning is life. An educational system fails when it attempts to give final, complete knowledge to students.

Final, complete knowledge does not exist. The school's duty is to motivate students, instilling in students the desire and love for further, unending learning and growth. Students who say that school gave them knowledge have attended the wrong institution. Those who remark that their schools inspired them toward further learning have attended the correct schools.

The difference between traditional and lifelong education is the difference between dehumanized and rehumanized, holistic, evolving, values learning. Traditional education teaches content only once without motivating students (and workers) to relearn. Lifelong learning is holistic and humanizing. Students are to be motivated to learn to grow, to appreciate values including the value of ongoing learning.

Workers can learn at the workplace as well as academe.[7] Corporations provide excellent lifelong learning opportunities.[8] General Motors Institute is the first corporation to provide an inhouse school for workers to learn.[9] Present growth rates of corporations providing schools for retraining would mean that eventually they will outnumber academic universities.[10] Americans are learning and relearning at work and school.

The learning process can occur at the workplace as workers periodically stop working and return to study. The learning process can intertwine with work such that workers go to work for certain days and to school at the workplace certain other days. Alternating between study and work need not mean a literal break of months in going to work.

2. Cycles

Workers must always learn. Lifelong education says that workers continually learn by alternating between study and work. They are human beings or as I put it, human becomings requiring continual education. The process philosophy of educatiion in terms of lifelong learning tells workers that they are students and human beings irreducible to workers. They learn throughout life in order to grow as human beings and workers. Learning throughout life overcomes the inert ideas that education ends at graduation and workers never study.

Lifelong learning blurs traditional education's distinction between student and worker. That distinction says that human beings start life as students attending a decade or two of school, and then graduate to become workers. Human beings are students only during their youth and early adulthood. Upon receiving their degrees, students overnight become workers and never again return to school as students.

This traditional view of learning indicates that students learn everything they need to know about work while attending school for the decade or two. Once students earn their diplomas, they no longer need to learn more because no more knowledge exists. School is a once-and-for-all activity. Graduation is the sign that learning is completed and students are now qualified to work without further learning until they retire. They need never return to school after graduation or retirement.

Process education teaches that workers need always return to school, even after retiring. Alfred North Whitehead points out[11] that professionals must produce but also have a life outside work. He does not mention retirement, but to have a life outside work before retiring implies that life is full after workers no longer work.

One way to learn about this is to learn that professionals engage in the work-cycle some of the time, and spend time in school during the study-cycle thinking about work. Workers should not spend their entire lives in the work-cycle. Human beings are irreducible to working as mathematicians and lawyers.[12] Human beings are irreducible to any field of work. They are basically learners who should continually learn about learning. Becoming increasing experienced in a career is good. Doing nothing more than gaining experience can have a bad side-effect. Workers can get to the point of ignoring ongoing education, the evolving nature of life, and the changes in their fields. Learning to be a mathematician, lawyer, or other professional lacking values are inert ideas. We overcome these inert ideas by realizing that we are fundamentally human becomings as well as workers.

The traditional view of work is that learning is completed before graduation. Ernest L. Boyer says the traditional idea of learning saw the degree as reflecting a finished education. "We had...15 or 20 years of formal learning..." and "...then 40 years of tedious work...." In this view, higher education "...was the time of finishing up before you entered the real world."[13] Formal learning occurred for the fifteen or twenty years, and no further education was necessary. The fifteen or twenty years of study taught students everything that they must know for work. When students entered the workforce upon graduation, they would always be workers and never again be called students. Entering the workforce signified that students were now well-educated, their knowledge and learning complete. Students were then only workers prepared and obligated to work for the remainder of their lives to earn a living. Ernest L. Boyer criticizes the traditional approach to learning and calls for lifelong learning.

We cannot divide human beings into student and worker, or life into the distinct times of study and work. Secretary of Health, Education, and Welfare, John W. Gardner points out that education is no longer restricted to what human beings do between the ages of six and...twenty-two.[14] From the perspective of John W. Gardner, learning is lifelong. Human beings are not students while studying for their degrees, and workers after earning their degrees. Inert ideas fragment people into students who do not work and workers who never learn. Lifelong learning's wholeness shows that workers are student-workers or worker-students.

Human beings comprise the student-worker, or worker-student continuum. Workers do not leave behind their identities as students. Students are not preparing for their diplomas as a sign of dropping their status as learners in order to take on a new, permanent identity as workers. Learning is lifelong, and workers always learn. Lifelong learning opposes the view of inert ideas that learning occurs only during formal education.

Alfred North Whitehead criticizes the idea that students are reducible to passive listening.[15] Inert ideas or dead knowledge are ideas that we feed to passive students. I call "inert careers" those that are in the traditional workforce when no change or evolution occurs in jobs. Workers in inert careers passively go to work each day and never consider their aims, purpose, meaning, or value as human beings. Inert learning is traditional education that assumes learning to be complete and fixed when students graduate. Even if students participate in learning until graduation, and do not continue to learn after earning their degrees, society would still consider them passive students no longer learning. Their knowledge is inert ideas. Education that continues throughout life assumes that workers are always learning and always students, and that jobs are constantly evolving.

From the perspective of Alfred North Whitehead, we must assume that students are alive throughout life.[16] Students continue to be learners after graduation and during work. They are always engaging in the learning process if we only allow them to do so. Students are not dead or passive. They are living human beings participating in the learning process at all times during life. The educational system's fundamental objective is to motivate and inspire students to want to learn after receiving their degrees.

Learning that is lifelong can appreciate the words of William Shakespeare from *Hamlet*. In this play, Hamlet is talking with Horatio and says that more things exist in heaven and earth than of which Horatio's philosophy dreams.[17] Horatio wants answers to questions. Hamlet is stating that life does not always have answers. Existence is an ever-evolving process. A process philosophy of education shows that more knowledge exists and will unfold that we can imagine. That evolutionary view attacks the perspective of traditional learning. Traditional education says learning is completed with earning the degree. From the perspective of traditional learning, nothing exists in heaven and on earth than our roughly twenty years of formal education tell us. A Shakespearean approach would be that knowledge and reality are always going to bring more knowledge than we can imagine.

The Shakespearean approach holds that reality, society, education, and human beings are an evolving whole. At any given point, we cannot imagine what will occur down the road. We know that we will evolve and learn things unheard of in the past and present. Formal learning until the age of twenty-five or so only introduces students to work and existence. After graduation, heaven and earth reveal newer ideas everyday. Workers must realize their worker-student identity and alternate between the two institutions of job and school. The Shakespearean view rejects the inert ideas that life and knowledge are static.

Learning throughout life involves the view that questions and answers occur at all times during life. Questions are not exhausted during formal education in the first twenty-two years of study. Newer questions arise everyday in life. Older questions are given newer interpretations and ways of being asked. Answers arise everyday. Lifelong learning gives new interpretations to existing answers, and clarifies what we thought we knew well.

Students as student-workers alternate between work and study. Ernest L. Boyer says students will return to school in "cyclical"[18] manner. Traditional learning says human beings attend school as students for roughly twenty years, and then graduate to become workers, who never again can be called students. From the perspective of Ernest L. Boyer, lifelong learning as a process philosophy of education offers the cyclical approach.

In cyclical education and work, students attend school for roughly twenty years and graduate. They enter the workforce. Their identity as students is never left behind. Workers are worker-students, or student-workers. Periodically, workers return to school to relearn about jobs and themselves. Workers alternate between work and study. Education becomes a cyclical activity along with work. Work and education go hand-in-hand. They are inclusive and never mutually exclusive. The inclusive approach that work and education are related rejects the inert ideas that school and work are mutually exclusive.

Work and study interrelate throughout life because reality and human beings are always evolving, always becoming. Human becomings are continually learning, growing, developing, and evolving toward higher and deeper states of understanding and humanity. Modern society and lifelong learning involve change and evolution.

Alfred North Whitehead[19] writes that modern society is one of change and novelty. Modern civilization or culture reflect a dynamic reality. People in a modern culture face new situations and challenges daily, and must learn to adapt to those ongoing conditions. Modern people are human beings or human becomings continually rethinking their nature and destiny. Alfred North Whitehead denies the validity of the static nature of ancient civilizations.

Ancient peoples held to the notion of the "fixed person for the fixed duties."[20] The ancients saw reality as a static entity involving inert ideas and not a dynamic, evolving process. They aimed for social cohesion. They accomplished their goals through maintaining tribal tradition. Ancient people performed their tasks by repeating what their gods had done. Persons in ancient culture performed their work in much the same manner for generations. Phenomenologist and historian of religion, Mircea Eliade, points this out in his work.[21]

When ancient tribes are asked by Eliade why they perform a task a certain way, they reply that they do so because the gods did this task a certain way.[22] The gods and ancestors sit, eat, hunt, engage in sex, and so on, in certain anatomical positions. The ancestors commanded that the tribe members do things in the same anatomical manner. Tribe members do things in a certain anatomic and procedural way because the Holy People performed those things in those ways in the first place. Ancient people refuse to change their ways of life and work because the gods first lived and worked in those anatomic ways.[23] As a result of tradition, ancient tribes taught their children to do all things the way that the gods had done.

Everything in ancient communities was fixed. Social cohesion was fundamental to the community. Innovation would change things, and the ancients did not wish anything to change. Any change would disrupt their community. Ancient cultures practiced inert ideas. Their practices reflected a stagnant universe which meant a denial of change and always held onto tradition.

When people are fixed in their social and economic situations, social and communal cohesion exists in the wrong manner. Tribes with all members holding to their traditions seem to be living a stable life. We may say that they lived in a static reality. Many of these tribes hated each other and saw themselves as the center of reality. Tribes considered the other tribes and communities as "them" and not part of a global "us." The rate at which cultures fought each other and practiced discrimination shows that their tribal identities consisted of hating and distrusting other communities.

I have shown above that Alfred North Whitehead compares change and learning (what we call lifelong learning) in modern cultures with the static world-views of ancient civilization. Similarly, I have noted that John W. Gardner and Ernest L. Boyer compare lifelong learning with modern society's static learning called the traditional educational system. Can anything in modern society be compared with ancient people? I believe that Western humanity's traditional learning is comparable with ancient cultures' learning. Both traditional learning and ancient tribal education see reality, knowledge, and human beings as static.

Let us consider Western civilization with ancient people. Western humanity follows the view of linear instead of cyclical history. The ancients believed in cyclical time. Tribal members continually returned to or repeated their ancestors' or gods' ways instead of seeing time and history marching forward. Ernest L. Boyer mentions lifelong learning as cyclical. The term cyclical does not automatically designate a static reality, and the term linear does not inevitably signify evolutionary and progressive knowledge.

Let me compare cyclical and linear thinking. I will show that while modern Western civilization believes in linear history, education and work can remain static. Linear history does not *ipso facto* signify progress and evolution. Ancient cultures repeated their gods' actions as narrated to them through tribal leaders. Ancient civilizations believed in cyclical time or history instead of linear history. Time never went forward for ancient people. They always existed in and returned to their gods' time (the beginning of the world) in order to do things. No knowledge or behavior existed other than what the gods had done. In our civilization prior to lifelong learning, the traditional idea that education was completed when receiving the degree, is similar to ancient cultures' notion of a static reality. Professors would tell students what to believe and not believe.

Comparing traditional education with ancient people seems strange. Everyone may believe that linear history means time marches on and society progresses. My point is that ancient people and our own traditional education believed that knowledge is static. By graduation time, students in traditional learning know everything they need in order to work. No further knowledge exists. Knowledge does not evolve. Work does not evolve. History is linear before the idea of lifelong learning. Linear history in traditional education means that students learn day by day what human beings have thought and developed for learning. Each day is a new, different day for growing older, for aging, but not evolving as human beings or becomings. Traditional learning and ancient tribes practice inert ideas of rejecting change and growth.

Students in traditional learning progressively, linearly learn everything by graduation. Each school day is a new day for learning. After graduation, they enter the work-cycle and produce without further learning until retirement. Work occurs in linear history or fashion. Each day is a new day for working, producing, earning more money, without the need to relearn skills or our human nature. Human beings evolve in the sense that they earn more, and change by aging. Knowledge is complete and does not evolve after graduation. Work remains intellectually static instead of evolving and demanding newer skills. Jobs remain the same in methods and knowledge.

Lifelong learning shows that graduation is the beginning of knowing, learning, and working. The work-cycle involves evolving work, knowledge, learning, and doing. As student go between work-cycle and learning-cycle, they alternate and go forward in evolving manner. Lifelong learning integrates cyclicity and linearity. Workers work during the work-cycle and return to school in the study-cycle. The work-cycle and study-cycle are then repeated in an evolving, forward, linear fashion toward the future. As we alternate between work and study, we learn a little bit more each time.

Ongoing education clarifies the things to which workers were introduced as students in undergraduate learning. Unfortunately, traditional education implies that introductory courses are the only introductions to knowledge. The implication is that an introductory courses provides the overview, and advanced undergraduate courses give the fuller, complete perspective in any field. Lifelong learning rejects the inert ideas that learning occurs only once and that workers never relearn jobs or life.

Ongoing education tells students and workers that learning before graduation is the introduction to a lifetime of learning. Advancing knowledge, never completed, continues after graduation. A process philosophy of education informs students that they are always being reintroduced to a field. Advanced studies cannot mean leaving behind the introductory perspectives. Advanced learning builds upon, refers to, and evolves the introductions.

The State University of New York (SUNY) at Stony Brook, and The Evergreen State College in the State of Washington are examples of what they term Learning Communities emphasizing lifelong learning. Wayne State University's College of Lifelong Learning maintains the Interdisciplinary Studies Program for ongoing education.

Programs and seminars help senior citizens to always learn. The Center for Older Adults at Fourth Presbyterian Church in Chicago abounds with numerous seminars, lectures, and other lifelong learning experiences for senior citizens. Blue Cross and Blue Shield of Illinois publishes *Life Times*, a monthly paper of news, the arts and sciences, and learning programs relevant to senior citizens. In Chicago the Department of Aging runs Life Enrichment Programs through many regional centers presenting seminars, meetings with authors, and a variety of health and recreational activities.

Ancient people returned to and never innovated the gods' ways of behaving. The gods' ways were taught by priests or other community leaders as infallible. Life was basically theological or religious, without any secular and human research, inquiry, or debate. Traditional education students learned everything in existence by graduation time, though they never returned to what any gods did. Students before lifelong learning were taught that human beings had developed existing knowledge, and that no further developments existed. We see religious and secular notions of static knowledge. The ancients depended on divinely inspired tradition and behavior; traditional education before lifelong education depended on human effort creating complete knowledge. From the perspective of lifelong learning, workers as students return to institution for relearning.

The learning process never concludes in complete knowledge. Roger Brown makes a good point about knowledge as evolution. We proceed from knowing a little to knowing a little bit more than we know, instead of going from total ignorance to complete knowledge.[24] Lifelong learning's process philosophy of education says formal education leading to a degree introduces us to some knowledge. We knew a little from the beginning of school, and learned more toward the end. We are always learning more. Total ignorance and complete knowledge are examples of inert ideas which lifelong learning overcomes. Lifelong learning means we always begin by knowing a little and evolve toward knowing a little more than we know at the start. We are never starting from scratch and proceeding toward complete knowledge. The conclusion has started from the beginning. We began by knowing something instead of knowing nothing.

From the perspective of Robert Maynard Hutchins, America has become and will continue to develop as a learning society.[25] We no longer stop learning at graduation and enter the workforce devoid of learning. Life is learning. Workers no longer remain in a job where no innovation can emerge. We see changes even in the most manual jobs. People who repair shoes see changes such as newer plastics and other materials. Carpenters, electricians, shipping and receiving workers, all notice and relearn changes in their fields. New products, materials, handling and transporting methods, and processes, contribute to innovative techniques and practices.

No aspect of undergraduate or graduate school is once-and-for-all. Undergraduate and graduate education present the outlines of work. Robert Maynard Hutchins argues that education is an ongoing process as human beings learn and develop.[26] His point is that the more sophisticated and advanced a society becomes, the more that culture involves a lifetime of learning. People do not attend school only in their younger years. The educational process is a dynamic, unending enterprise extending throughout life.

Robert Maynard Hutchins indicates that an educational system exists to continually improve society.[27] As students graduate with their degrees and enter the workforce, they perform at a certain basic level of productivity. Throughout their lives they must return to school in order to relearn fundamentals, and learn new skills and ideas that will make life better. Process education helps us discover more of ourselves and reality. A dynamic educational system is part of ongoing reality. Reality is never a stagnant, fixed entity. The world is constantly unfolding as a unified whole which gives meaning and direction to everyone.

A lifetime of work and ongoing learning help workers explicate and develop that outline of work. No education can provide undergraduates or graduates with the complete knowledge required of any career. Complete knowledge may never exist. Reality is an ongoing, evolutionary process. The learning system as an evolving reality of values gives us daily a little bit more of an insight into our holistic nature.

From the perspective of lifelong learning's process education, society consists of the evolving work-cycle and study-cycle. Each cycle can occur by itself, or might intertwine with the other cycle. If the cycles are distinct, workers work for a year or two and then leave work in order to attend school for months or a year. They reenter the work-cycle and work for a year or so until the next study-cycle. If the work-learning cycles interrelate, workers will be in a position to go to work and than return to school during the same week, month, or year. Workers would not need to work for long periods of time without schooling.

3. Scholarship Evolves

In traditional learning, undergraduates would read material once, have one shot at understanding it, and pass tests to prove that they understand the texts. Traditional learning assumes that a set quantity of ideas and interpretations exist, and students need to grasp these within the semester or quarter's time that is given them. Once students read and complete their assignments, schools presumed that students have no more need to reread books later. Students who pass the exams have completely understood their assignments. Those who do not pass the exams will need to retake the course to gain complete understanding of the topic.

From the perspective of traditional learning, students cannot gain more understanding from books and articles they have read while undergraduates because knowledge, interpretation, and so on never evolve. In later life, if students discuss what they were taught as undergraduates and perhaps even graduate students, their answer is that they studied a book or group of books, and came to know certain knowledge. The assumption is that no knowledge evolves. What they learned as undergraduates was all that they need to know thereafter. Lifelong learning criticizes that notion.

Entering the work-cycle means we return to relearn many things which continue as basics, and learn new things. As we progress through the cycles of work and study, we always learn more. Our knowing never stops, and we never know everything. Even if we relearn some things which do not change, we learn new perspectives and interpretations of them and gain greater appreciation for their lasting values. If certain literature are classics, we reread them to gain better understanding of their content. We restudy basic principles in the arts and sciences to evolve in our understanding of reality. When we say reality evolves, we could mean that basic principles or theories unfold in their complexity and generality.

As I read books, I notice what authors say in their introductions concerning the evolving nature of their research. I present below a few random samples of the evolving nature of books and research.

David W. Neubauer says that the fifth edition of his *America's Courts and the Criminal Justice System* "offers a current perspective on a continually evolving subject—the criminal court process."[28] His book is only a current, transitional view which will change in the near future. Society is changing. The judicial, legal, criminal justice, and law enforcement systems are changing. Our knowledge about human nature and behavior is evolving. All this is having an impact on the courts and criminal justice system. The evolving criminal court system rejects the inert ideas of static judicial, legal, criminal justice, and law enforcement systems. These systems are constantly changing and interrelating.

Carl E. Lutrin and Allen K. Settle indicate that the second edition of their

American Public Administration: Concepts & Cases, aims to keep up with vast changes taking place in American public administration.[29] Issues about the government's relation to private enterprise, the role of government in helping people in need, Church and State problems, and a myriad of other dilemmas are forcing changes in the ways we think about what is public and private. American public administration consists of wholeness and growth instead of inert ideas. I now turn to the idea of cybernetics or control theory.

Years of innovations changed and evolved the idea of control theory.[30] Every subject-matter in the arts and sciences is rapidly changing. Norbert Weiner points out that the second edition of his *Cybernetics* is a response to the need to clarify and expand on the first edition. Authors and their critics may be satisfied with what a book says and how it handles various questions. We may be certain that newer research, thinking, probing, and serendipitous events will shed unexpected light on any topic. Authors are not stupid if their books are later clarified. Authors are evolving and gaining newer and better insight. Weiner rejects the notion of inert ideas as he writes that cybernetics is an ever-changing field.

Authors realize that since their initial book has been published, clarification of terms and improved precision of an idea's role becomes imperative. Often, the book has reached and influenced wider audiences than were anticipated. Richard A. Johnson, Fremont E. Kast, and James E. Rosenzweig write their third edition of *Theory and Management of Systems* due to the need for clarifying and making more precise the ever-widening acceptance of systems thinking.[31] When Richard A. Johnson, Fremont E. Kast, and James E. Rosenzweig wrote their first edition, they did not anticipate how ubiquitous the idea of systems would become. Their third edition attempts to show more precisely the various levels of systems analysis. Values and wholeness in the evolving ideas of systems thinking reject inert ideas of static management systems.

Philosophers can point to two works by Ludwig Wittgenstein exemplifying evolution. His *Tractatus Logico-Philosophicus* attempted to portray a universe reducible to the sum of simple parts or elements.[32] His subsequent *Philosophical Investigations* contributes to philosophical literature by rejecting summative thinking, and calling for a holistic approach to philosophy.[33] Having completed his *Tractatus*, Wittgenstein continued to think, be bothered by the analytic, context-free approach, and evolve his ideas about the ultimate nature of reality. He accepted and later rejected inert ideas as his thinking embraced wholenss and values.

I consider another insight. Authors like to conclude writing a book by statements from themselves. Readers infer that books are relatively complete and authors having said all they can say for the moment. Authors give the attitude that they are the authorities to judge what their books indicate. I respect and expect that attitude. I do not expect authors to conclude their books by saying that they do not know what they are talking about, or that their book contributes nothing to knowledge. Should their opinions evolve or new research mean another book, the authors are probably the best judges of the current work. David G. Barnum concludes a book on the Supreme Court with the point that whether the role of the Court is satisfactory now rests with the readers.[34]

David G. Barnum is concluding his work by stating the research and background he has completed and presented to readers. Readers must carefully read and analyze the book in terms of David G. Barnum's extensive research and deep understanding of the issues concerning the Supreme Court. His insights and scholarship comprise a framework which readers must take seriously in order to make judgments about the book. He understands that every book is a dialogue between authors and readers, between authors and an evolving society.

His statement about the readers' right to consider the Supreme Court's role makes explicit what other authors either assume or will learn in time. Authors will see that events will change their books and compel subsequent revisions. David G. Barnum is prepared for such change, and verbally anticipates readers' role in contributing to revisions of his book. Readers will read his book and think about the Court's role. They must do so within the context and information he has established, since he is the authority writing the book.

Authors write books as revisions of earlier works. Authors may also write a book evolving from previous articles. In the process, authors' ideas change. Norman Perrin attempted to revise a number of religious essays and publish them as a book. In attempting the revisions, he found that his own thinking had changed, developed, and matured as he engaged in dialogue with Paul Ricoeur and others. The result was a complete rewriting of his original papers.[35]

Research evolves. Students having studied works in undergraduate and gradute school, and instructors having taught from them, can return to school to rethink the topics and read the newer editions and clarifications. Knowledge about everything including criminal justice, religion, administration, and cybernetics is continually developing. Authors need to clarify concepts and add newer ideas.

Students read books during college. Traditionally, once they have read these books, schools assume that students no longer need to reread them or their read their newer editions. Students supposedly no longer need to think about varying interpretations of these books. Ongoing learning disputes that scenario. Once students graduate and become workers, they need to return to school to reread books that have not been expanded or revised. Their rereading and comments can influence authors to do another book. Students should also read updated versions of books, and books that are rewritings of previously published articles.

Only the most arrogant authors will conclude their books by stating that no change or revision is necessary for their work. Arrogant authors are a prime example of inert scholars. Authors need not conclude their books by explicitly inviting reader input. They need understand that every book is always in a state of revision. If human beings are human becomings, then all research including books and articles can be updated as soon as they are published. Research within the context of human becomings is an on-going process.

4. Continual College

A. A. Liveright suggests that the future school will be a college or university of continual education.[36] We think of lifelong learning occurring in a college or university, but continue to call these institutions as colleges or universities. We imply that the institutions are not for evolving, holistic values. A. A. Liveright believes we must include "continuing" or a synonym in the terms "college" or "university." He argues that at the least, a university will include a college of continuing education. The idea of a college of continuing education involves a wholeness rejecting inert ideas that a college education does not continue after graduation.

I find it instructive that ongoing education occurs more often than we think in attending church or synogogue. I have attended Baptist, Armenian Orthodox, Armenian Protestant, Jewish, and Presbyterian services. In each case, clergy refer to the same scriptures as they did years before. The difference is that scriptures are mentioned in their relevant to a contemporary context. Appropriately different interpretations and explications are given. Most services I have attended have been Presbyterian, since I have mostly been a member of that Protestant Denomination. I recall that from time to time, clergy refer to scriptures that were read years before, and read them in light of current, differing situations.

My point is that the modern clergy do not tell their worshippers and visitors that a scripture will be read only once during their lifetime. From the practical perspective, such reading might be possible since sufficient scriptures exist in the Bible and Torah for each to be read only once in a generation. From my experience, clergy are more judicious. Over a period of years, they repeat scripture passages and give them different twists and relate them to various circumstances. The modern church and synogogue is a learning religous society. Wholeness and values in religion overcome the inert ideas that we read a given passage of scripture in church or synogogue only once.

For the past ten years, I have attended annual Passover Seders in conjunction with my church, Fourth Presbyterian of Chicago, and Temple Sinai. I notice over the years that the Seder contains roughly the same songs and prayers each year. Each year, we repeat the same words, but refer to different appropriate contexts and world-events.

Reminding ourselves of past horrors such as the Holocaust does not mean we are not progressing or evolving. We must remind ourselves of evils that have occurred and that could recur. We then ask ourselves how future evil can be prevented. The knowledge that evil has occurred is often sufficient to realize that we must prevent it in the future. However, even human becomings need continual reminders that evil must be monitored and its potential never forgotten.

In academia, we can refer to recurring themes, and give fresh interpretations to past events. Our nature evolves. Our understanding and knowledge evolve. We may and ought to speak of the same ideas and connect them to our present contexts in relevant ways.

Workers need to see themselves as workers and human beings always capable of and engaging in relearning. The workplace separates specialists into their fields. Workplaces also do not entirely isolate workers from each other. During the working cycle, people from various professions often relate. A mathematician relates to secretaries, other intellectuals on nondepartmental committees, the administration, family life, and people outside work who provide grants. Lawyers relate to clients, to lawyers in subspecialties, and so on. In the work-cycle and study-cycle, every professional or worker should learn their human and nonspecialist identity as well as their working title.

5. Reunion or Lifelong Reuniting

Colleges and universities have a process which has not yet been fully developed for lifelong learning. I speak of the reunion. Reunions are times when alumni return for fun and various activities on campus. I believe the reunion could evolve into an institutional time of returning to relearn.

Reunion means workers were once united as students. Students earned their degrees and enter the work-cycle to work as specialists in their respective fields. They return to be reunited not as specialists, but as students and human beings in an institution providing values and not just goods and typical services.

The reunion tells us that we learned physics, chemistry, the liberal arts at a particular cultural location. Students did not just study general and specialized education. Students learned at Harvard, Princeton, MIT, and so on. Each college and university is a place founded by human beings during cultural events. Knowledge is embodied in people and culture, and irreducible to cognition. Embodiment is not relativism. Physics at MIT is more difficult than at a community college or many universities. My point is that physics or any subject is telling students the same thing regardless of location.

Relearning means that workers return to school to be reunited with other specialists in order to rethink different professions. Workers wish to be one with each other in order to evolve and relearn about change. In the work-cycle, workers are going to work to produce. In the study-cycle, different specialists return to school to see why, what, and how they have been producing.

Lifelong learning as a process philosophy of education reveals human beings as evolving, holistic, values. No student is completely learned upon graduation. No professional is completely learned at retirement. No worker is totally competent at retirement. No worker is only a worker. No student is only a student. Learning to learn is fundamental to work, specialized study, and our human nature. We are a learning human being, a human becoming.

The high school, college, and other kinds of reunion can be articulated and further explicated within the context of lifelong learning. Workers may return to their campuses for ongoing rehumanization, re-socialization, re-grouping with their former classmates. Reunion is a perfect time for workers to catch up. They can learn the latest ideas within their professions, the most recent innovations concerning new professions, and become reacquainted with former classmates comprising an ongoing social group. Reunions need not mean travelling to the actual campus.

With local clubs throughout the nation, frequent mini-reunions or local get-togethers bring together graduates from the same school. The Chicago Harvard club can be a model for various colleges and universities. Harvard graduates can reunite with those in the Chicago or other local area club who attended their school. Their reunion can begin as a social and cultural function, ongoing reorientation about Harvard, themselves, the world, and proceed toward more intellectual matters. Reunions become communions. Workers commune or form a community among themselves. Such reunions would not imply that Harvard graduates need not commune with other people. A reunion suggests that Harvard held or continues to hold a special place in the hearts and minds of its graduates. Having been introduced to learning at Harvard, a Harvard or MIT club becomes the focal point of local, evolving, professional and cultural development.

Throughout their lives, alumni can and should socialize or associate with co-workers who attended different colleges. Their college reunions can provide a foundation for ongoing associations and networking. The potential of reunions for becoming a vibrant aspect of lifelong learning is yet to be fully realized. Sports, dinners, and other activities are traditional aspects of the reunion. Workers return to their Alma Mater to see their team play against other teams from other colleges. Workers return to their campuses to see, dine, and otherwise socialize with former classmates and former instructors.

Reunions can be more fully articulated as lifelong learning events. The reunion is telling workers that their productive identity is only part of life. Study was a union or wholeness prior to entering the workforce. Entering the workforce was a diversification or specialization. Economics meant a dis-unity or non-unity. Holistic economics involves a reuniting or nonspecialization. Holistic productivity involves a re-humanizing of the laborer or specialist. We once again see ourselves as studying, thinking, relearning and not just doing, producing, or earning a living. Once again, during reunion, workers become rehumanized as they share with former classmates their common, pre-instrumental, fundamentally whole or humanistic existence.

The college reunion can be combined with freshmen orientation. Reunions may be called lifelong reorientations. As workers return to their campuses, they can be said to be reoriented as human beings and workers. The reorientation-reunion can mean opportunities for growth for incoming students as well as returning workers. Lifelong learning can extend, articulate, and explicate the meaning of orientation as well as reunion.

Lifelong orientation means students are oriented or introduced to academe, and then continually reoriented through reunions. They are oriented toward themselves as human beings, as human becomings who will spend time working. Reorientation and reunion would involve rehumanization as workers return to understand more of their worker-student identities. Humanization does not and cannot occur only once in life. We need to rehumanize life, work, education, and society on an ongoing basis. Humanizing ourselves once and then forgetting about it assumes that all human beings will respect our efforts. Process of existence is an ongoing venture of lifelong rehumanization. The holistic ideas of reunion and communing with former classmates overcomes the inert ideas that graduates should never return to their colleges and universities.

6. Improving Lifelong Learning

We can and should improve upon existing lifelong learning. I wish to imbed ongoing education within our society.

Lifelong learning typically involves adults or workers returning to school to relearn. Relearning or ongoing learning is good, but insufficient. Lifelong learning implies that people are only learners disembodied from families. Workers are human beings. Their human nature means they are part of a social structure. Many workers are parents. Ongoing education should be more than an opportunity for the adult to relearn.

An improved ongoing learning system helps parents and children to relearn together. When working parents return to school, part of their program ought be to relearn with their children. Their children may be studying in elementary, middle, or high school. The children may be attending college or a university. If the children are studying in different schools, the parents might be able to participate in some limited manner with each child.

By participating with the offspring, parents can relearn what they had originally been taught as children, but do the relearning at the time that their own children are learning for the first time. Parents are able then to see what their children are facing. Rosalind Rossi[37] tells how Chicago Mayor, Richard M. Daley, urges parents to accompany their children to school on the first day of classes. Daley has the correct direction. He should expand on his idea and propose parental lifelong learning seminars so parents can attend schools from time to time with their children. Employers should cooperate and participate in such programs.

This type of lifelong learning also helps parents better understand their offsprings and the childrens' problems. If the children study new material in any level that differs from what the parents learned growing up, fathers and mothers have a better idea of different things with which their children are be challenged.

If the children study different ideas in colleges, parents can attend and learn how newer ideas affect all members of the family. When college and university students are studying specialties differing from those in which the fathers or mothers are working, parental participation helps parents understand and relate to fields other than ones in which they earned degrees. Should children follow their parents' footsteps in a field, parents can help their offspring study the material to the extent that the information is similar to what the parents studied.

Lifelong learning becomes more than workers or adults returning to school to relearn. Parents and children grow together, and parents are able to see how their offspring are doing. Ongoing learning with parents and children participating provides parents with the opportunity give help where needed for their children. Since parents are already working, they have the chance to help their children find a job after graduation. The children may be able to follow the parents' career to some extent, or benefit from parental advice about finding appropriate professions. Consortiums including corporations, college and universities, and schools ranging from elementary to high school, can mean a network for ongoing family study and work. Lifelong learning through parent-child programs would be an excellent means of helping parents learn and relearn parenting. Parenting becomes part of lifelong learning.

Two

REHUMANIZING DISTANCE LEARNING

Students can learn in the classroom, Internet, and interactive distance learning. My present chapter concerns the humanizing process within interactive distance learning. I am not endorsing or criticizing interactive distance learning. Interactive distance learning probably has a place in education. The role of interactive distance learning is not my aim in this chapter. My aim is only to show that interactive distance learning puts technology second to the need for instructors to use their equipment for dignifying students.

Interaction in distance learning must be lifelong. Interaction between instructors and students and among students never stops. Teachers and students should always interact. The teacher-student relation in interactive distance learning is a dynamic, evolving process continuing as a perennial goal. Interaction is fundamental to distance learning and technology.

Technology is part of the interactive-distance learning continuum. Students need community or interaction in distance learning. Community humanizes distance learning technology. Communing human beings learn through distances and technology. Distance learning is irreducible to technology. Distance learning reduced to technology becomes inert distance learning. Inert distance learning is failure to develop community between teacher and students. Students in distance learning are first and always holistic persons in a community. Distance learning without interaction means the inert ideas of distance learning.

1. Interaction

Alfred North Whitehead[1] and Paulo Freire[2] say that students are active human beings. Teachers must never treat students as passive receptacles to be filled with inert ideas. Students are participants in a dynamic teacher-student relationship. Alfred North Whitehead was speaking about students in the classroom. Interactive distance learning implements the Whiteheadian notion of students as alive through technological processes.

Martin Buber says that we must consider each other as Thou[3] and never as It. Thou means that other human beings are to be dignified as am I. Every person requires respect. No human being is an object. Respecting students as alive, as does Alfred North Whitehead, means dignifying them as Thou, as does Martin Buber. The passive view of students reduce each student to an It.

Interactive distance learning consists of highly complex electronic equipment in a control room, origin site, and two or more distant sites. I will not go into detail about the layout and equipment. My aim is only to show the human purpose of the equipment: interaction is necessary for the successful process of distance learning.

Instructors, usually with students present, teach in the origin site. Origin and distant sites differ only in terms of semantics. Both sites are similar in design. An origin site can be a distant site, and *vice versa*, depending on where the instructors will be teaching. The origin site is called the origin site because professors are present and do the teaching in this location. The teaching originates in the origin site. Students are usually present because the origin site was initially a classroom which the school converted into an interactive distance learning room. If the school builds a building with origin sites, officials want the room to have students with the instructors. Interactive distance learning does not mean that instructors must be the only ones in the origin site. The presence of instructors means that some students should be in the same room in order to have immediate, physical contact with instructors.

The origin site transmits the teaching to two or more distant sites. Distant sites are physically the same kind of rooms as origin sites. We call them distant sites because during the teaching, only students are present in the distant sites. Distant sites can one day become origin sites and origin sites the distant sites when a professor with students is assigned to what had been a distant site. Distant site students view and technologically interact with the teacher and students at the origin site, and with students in other distant sites participating in a given course.

Each site or classroom has television monitors and cameras. Distant site students view (origin site) teachers and students, and students in other distant sites. Teachers and students (at the origin site) view students at distant sites.

Viewers must look into cameras next to monitors to make eye contact with those viewed. Technology brings about minimal optic interaction by allowing all to view each other. Cameras facilitate deeper optic interaction by allowing eye contact with those viewed. Professors and students do not dignify each other simply through viewing one another. People dignify each other as they look into the camera to make eye contact with the persons being viewed.

As we dignify students whom we view, we acknowledge the Whiteheadian notion that the students are alive. Dignifying students by making eye contact with them also brings in Martin Buber's notion of the other person as a thou. Making eye contact with students enables the viewer to dignify students as a Thou. All cameras are capable of being moved or turned. Professors can turn them or zoom in on students. I mention this shortly.

A camera is in the ceiling above the instructors. This camera allows professors to write on an overhead, and on paper on their desk or podium. The writing is transmitted to distant students. Professors can, if they or their students prefer, write on blackboards behind them. Instructors can make this camera zoom in on students when students are talking and others want to see and not just hear them.

Fax machines, photocopiers, and telephones are placed near instructors' tables. Instructors and students fax and phone each other. Professors and students may also photocopy documents. Phones are used for emergencies, routine but necessary contact between sites, and for privacy. Professors wishing to talk privately with distant students dial those students' number and speak with them so that the others will not hear the conversation.

A control panel on the professors' desks allows them to select who appears on the monitors, pan cameras in their and distant sites, zoom in on students, and so on. These actions constantly acknowledge humanity and dignity of students and professors. When students appear on monitors, students and professors viewing them can make eye contact with them by looking into appropriate cameras. By zooming cameras closer to students or themselves, professors dignify the person appearing on the monitor.

Dignifying students in distance learning should be minute-, hour-, course-, and lifelong. Professors respect students not just once or twice during class, but throughout the session. They dignify students in any class, and every time a class is taught. Making eye contact with who appears on monitors, having cameras to allow students and professors to be on monitors, are part of the ongoing rehumanization of distance learning.

When Alfred North Whitehead says students are alive, he is indicating that student need and want to participate in the learning experience. They are not passive receptacles for data or inert ideas. In interactive distance learning, lifelong return to community between teacher and student means students are physically alive. They want and need teachers to make eye-contact with them. Students need instructors to answer their questions, send and receive faxes as needed, and talk with them on phones as required.

Students in the classroom are alive in that they need to participate in the learning process and be motivated to relearn in the future. Distance learning students are alive in that they require at least visual, vocal, fax, and phone interaction with students and faculty.

Elimination of interaction from distance learning reduces educational processes to inert ideas of passive learning. Interactive distance learning is necessary for rehumanizing even the most sophisticated electronic school technology.

2. Security

Security is as much a part of interactive distance learning as of the traditional classroom. Interactive distance learning complicates security. Professor are burdened moreso than in regular classes. Their burden is due to students in distant sites being without instructors or people to watch the distant situation for emergencies. Responsibility for their safety rests with the instructors in the site of origin. Safety of the students in the instructors' presence is typically easy. When an emergency occurs where instructors are, instructors know immediately that school security officers must be contacted. Safety for those in distant sites is trickier.

Instructors see only what is on the screens before them. Rehumanization of distance learning technology means instructors need cameras at distant sites which can move or pan around to show as much as possible of the distant classroom. Computer boxes or panels on instructors' tables allow instructors to pan the distant site cameras. Panning is necessary for routine reasons of seeing that things are fine in the distant site. Panning is especially vital to see the reasons of an emergency if the incident or danger occurs out of the camera's current range. Cameras do not move automatically. I doubt that cameras should be automatically moving. Automatic mobility relegates panning to the camera and takes this responsibility away from the professor.

Instructors can continually switch the scenes on the monitors on any site. Scenes should never be the same for a long period of time. Students in distant sites deserve and want to see students and professors at origin sites.

The humanizing element in distance learning is a process philosophy of education. Rehumanization is lifelong in distance learning. Instructors need to interact with students in all courses, during all years of teaching. Distance learning is a process of switching monitor scenes from site to site, student to student, close-up to farther away, and panning the cameras. Distance learning requires continual rehumanization through speaking with as many students as possible, trying to say their names, phoning when necessary, faxing when appropriate or needed, and monitoring emergencies.

An holistic approach to distance learning is lifelong. Instructors must always be on the alert for anything that appears dangerous or threatening at a distant site. Checking monitors, if students at a distant site express concern through facial movement, instructors should immediately ask if something is wrong. If unusual sounds or scenes emerge, instructors must inquire about what is happening. Inattention to students' safety reduces classroom security to inert ideas where pupils are considered only objects and not human beings.

3. Teaching Tools

Instructors need to understand that they are teaching through television. Their speech, and particularly writing, are being electronically, mediately transmitted to distant sites. Mediacy sometimes distorts or otherwise changes things for the worst.

Instructors should always ask distant students if the students can easily read what is being written, especially on an overhead. A pen, pencil, marker, certain color of paper, and so on, may need to be changed to make the transmitted visual image improved. A green felt-tip marker may not show up as well as a black felt-tip marker. Instructors should ask students if they are able to read what is being written with a certain colored marker. If students have difficulty reading the material, instructors must have other colored markers ready to be used so students can read the material better.

Distant site students may want instructors to write on the board and not on paper on the desk. Instructors should generally try to honor those requests. Their task is to make it as easy and reasonable as possible for students to learn.

Instructors should always be alert as to what to do with the control box before them. Their fingers should move around on the box approximately as though they are typing slowly. The experienced professors arrive at their origin sites early enough to test the equipment. Should problems arise, instructors must then contact their control rooms for help from technicians.

Generally speaking, instructors can reach control rooms by talking into their microphones or dial the phone. Microphones can often reach the control room. They are generally connected to the control rooms so the instructors with sudden technical problems can quickly reach the technicians simply by calling out the need for technical help. Otherwise, professors can pick up a phone in the classroom and dial the control room number.

In some instances, instructors have the option of reaching control rooms at the distant sites. Origin and distant sites, differing in name only, have control rooms near them. Technicians near the origin site might not know about or be unable to diagnose or correct a distant site's problems. Instructors or technicians then attempt to contact technicians at the distant site.

4. Before Interaction

Public or educational television is technology without wholeness, rehumanization, or process philosophy of education. Students view professors without be able to ask questions, relate, or communicate with faxes and phones.

Public television aims at educational and cultural programming. People can tune in to commercial television for news and entertainment. Commercial television asks corporate sponsors to give money for news and entertainment in return for allowing the companies to sell their products on the air. Public television receives funds from taxes and contributions. Those funds enable public television to be commercial-free and concentrate on educating the public.

Education through public television involves teachers to stand in a studio and lecture through a television camera. Teachers are the only people in the studio aside from the technicians in the control room. Public television teachers teach a number of subjects taken from the arts and sciences. Teaching on public television to a mass audience carries a problem. No interaction exists between teacher and students.

Interactivity is impossible when teachers attempt to reach an audience of hundreds of thousands of viewers. People watching the program can only listen to the lecture and hope that they can keep up with the instructors. No way exists for students to ask questions. Students who passively watch a program are not participating as human beings engaged in the learning process. Passive listening and watching do not constitute learning.

Interactive distance learning changes that one-way teaching method. The changes humanizes distance learning. Even in distance learning, lifelong learning's process philosophy of education demonstrates that continual rehumanization is possible and necessary. Distance learning through television is irreducible to television and related electronic technology.

5. Technology Without Interaction

Technology can be used for ill. Educators and others can get carried away by technology and assume that equipment, even the most sophisticated, should replace interaction and sensitivity. Rehumanizing distance learning through student-teacher interactivity eliminates the inert ideas of value-free distance education.

Martha W. Thomas says[4] that business teleconferences fail when we put technology above the message. Her words apply to all interactive distance communication. The most sophisticated technology is only hardware and software. Instructors, businesspeople, and others involved in telecommunications must continually be sensitive to their audiences. Reliance on technology as the only way to get a message across will result in disaster.

Technology can help us electronically reach distant audiences. Only our values and sensitivity to others can bring success to any educational or other telecommunication. Technology is the electronic means to foster the interaction that can dignify distant students and others.

The world's most advanced, speedy, sophisticated, and otherwise state-of-the-art technology for distance communication and learning is useless if not properly used. Instructors who do not make eye contact with students, refuse to use phones and faxes when necessary, and otherwise fail to respond to student needs to participate, will fail in distance learning. The best equipment only transmits sights, sounds, and documents among students and teachers. Technology in interactive distance learning guarantees only that we will see and hear each other, and receive documents quickly. The equipment does not mean that instructors can do as they please in ignoring students.

The state-of-the-art television monitor, camera, system, and so on is inadequate. Technology is part of the teaching method. A camera which transmit the clearest picture in the world requires human beings to communicate with other human beings. Monitors that help students and teachers view the most advanced and sharp images are only revealing pictures. How instructors relate to students is fundamental to the most advanced machinery.

Distance learning without an ongoing sense of community between teacher and student reminds me of commercial television and values. The most sophisticated television sets do nothing for society if the programs are worthless. State-of-the-art home television can present violence and other desirable pictures to the family, especially to the children. If we are to hook televisions, computers, telephones, and faxes into a giant media network, our values and not technology will determine if society decays or advances.

Reducing learning to technology means that education is a dehumanized set of inert ideas where students are nothing more than physical bodies. Interactive distance learning provides a measure of dignity for electronic education.

6. Conclusion

Technology is neither inherently good or bad. In any telecommunication, values allow communicators to succeed or fail. Adequate electronics and physics are important for sound infrastructure. Any infrastructure is for human beings. Distance learning must be interactive to allow for interaction between student and teacher. Teachers must be willing to encourage student participation. Instructors must also be sensitive toward student needs and issues. If interactive distance learning is to be used, the fundamental requirement is how teachers will prevent inert ideas and use the technology to enhance the living, evolving student-teacher relationship.

Three

REHUMANIZING EDUCATIONAL LOCATION

My previous chapter shows how we can and must rehumanize distance learning. Television monitors enable students to view instructors and each other in different locations. Cameras are for making eye contact between everyone. Microphones for conversation among all. Faxes, phones, and photocopy machines facilitate privacy when needed, and communication at all times. The Internet is another option for learning. Professors teach online as their students are perceiving information off their own computers. We should not assume that interactive distance learning or the Internet can and should replace the traditional classroom.[1] To eliminate the classroom would mean inert ideas of learning. All of us need a sense of physical place. People live in neighborhoods, cities, and nations.

Inside learning, the classroom should be a lifelong option. The classroom is space; the Internet and interactive distance learning connect distant spaces. I will not detail the techniques and ideas about the Internet even in the general sense that I mentioned interactive distance learning in Chapter One. My present chapter justifies the classroom or space as the location where most learning should occur. I then indicate the problem of the philosophy of using the Internet and even interactive distance learning.

1. Classrooms Always Primary

Before people get carried away by technology, the Internet, and even interactive distance learning, they must understand the need for the classroom. Kelly McCollom[2] refers to efforts by Joseph Glover to push for students on a campus to learn primarily in the classroom and not on the Internet (or presumably even interactive distant learning).

The classroom gives students a sense of being together with each other and the intructors. People are social human beings, not viewers, eyes, voices, or other techniques or body parts. Sociologist of work, Fred Davis,[3] would concur that values and wholeness mean that a classroom with teachers and students present manifests a sociology of learning. Technology reduces the learning process to a more crass situation of perception without involvement.

Classrooms constitute an immediate experience. Television and the Internet comprise an electronic and false immediacy. Electronic instruments represent a mediated immediacy. The instrument is the mediation which allows the pseudo immediacy to occur.

Why do we have the Internet and interactive distance learning? These two ideas come to us a few decades after urban sprawl began. More dangerously, they appear with the notion that people like to opt for getting into the car and drive instead of walking one block to the "distant" corner drugstore. Any distance between our homes and another building, even perhaps across the street, becomes a long distance to overcome. This becomes the topic for my next section.

2. Urban Sprawl and Any Distance

Consider Hinduism and Buddhism. The Hindus are polytheists. They believe in many gods. Each god serves a particular purpose, and requires considerable ritual. The Buddhists saw that polytheism and ritualism do not bring joy and contentment. Hindu society had poverty and lower classes in misery while the upper classes or castes lived in luxury and ritualism. Buddhism reacted against ritualism and eliminated the gods.

Hinduism believes that atonement comes through mediacy. Mediacy in Hinduism means lots of ritual. Atonement is never immediate or personal. Salvation comes through spending much time doing ritual, performing acts. These are externals. Buddhism says that atonement is immediate or aritualistic. We find meaning going within instead of doing things from without.

In urban sprawl, we spend time going through spaces to arrive at a school or traditional classroom. The corner drugstore is a long way from home only because the store is not physically contiguous with a person's home. Our society has fragmented any space outside homes as blocks of land or space to overcome in getting to a destination. Urban sprawl involves the notion that residential, commercial, recreational, and other locations must exist distances too long for walking in a few moments.

We have substituted religious ritualism with travel and technological ritualism or mediacy. Going from where we are to where we wish to go takes time. Often our starting point is our home, and our destination is across the street. The sooner we arrive, the faster we travel, the more "immediately" we arrive. With learning, shopping, and so on, the computer and television bring distances closer.

Distance learning says that students can remain in a location near their homes and receive an educatioin. They do not need to spend time travelling over spaces to get to a distant school. The internet says something more powerful. Students can stay at home, in one room, in front of a computer, and learn from distances. Philosophically, online learning becomes solipsistic. Persons sit alone at their computers and "communicate" with those at the other end. They communicate with "others" but do so neurologically, reducing themselves to seeing print on the screen.

We replace theological polytheism with urban polytechnology. If Hindus have many gods, each for a different purpose, we have many technologies (cars, high speed trains, jet aircraft, buses, etc.) for travelling long distances. Travelling long distances is necessary for certain purposes including vacations, certain sales jobs, and so on. We need not travel speedily over long distances for everyday learning, shopping, socializing, recreation, and so on. Learning, shopping and other human activities are part of the total human being in a holistic environment. That environment should be a person's immediate neighborhood.

Our society replaces Buddhist nontheism with technological immediacy. Buddhism teaches that atonement and meaning are immediate and never reducible to ritualism. Salvation comes from inwardness and not external gods and rites. We are saying that the Internet and distance learning are for as much education as possible, bringing distant libraries and so on to the student with the click of a mouse. The click is technological or mediated immediacy. Society has to manufacture the equipment for us to get immediate access through the computer.

The idea of the traditional classroom means that we need to stretch the space between us and the computer to comprise a regular classroom. The classroom as interpersonal, social immediacy is then between the electronic immediacy of the Internet (no space to travel) and electronic mediacy of cars and so on (lots of spaces in urban sprawl to travel).

I find it necessary to speak briefly of Judaism. The Jews reject polytheism and ritualism (salvation requires many gods and much ritual), and atheism. Judaism gives the world monotheism. One God and only necessary ritual comprise the road to salvation. Christianity (and other Faiths) must take Judaism into account as a powerful Faith, and by analogy, the idea of rejecting both polytheism's ritualism (extreme mediacy) and nontheism's aritualism (extreme immediacy).

Readers will argue that even monotheism, as in Catholicism, can consist of lots of ritualism. I would point out that the Protestant Reformation was an attempt to prune excess ritual (not ritual) and find meaning in a given ritual. The Reformation was not to end ritual and theism.

The process philosophy of lifelong learning means that we need to always return to the classroom's immediacy, rejecting urban sprawl's fragmentation of space and the Internet's false immediacy all but denying the legitimacy of travelling even short distances. Fragmentation of space requires technical tools of mediacy including cars to overcome blocks of space. The Internet's technical abilities give us immediacy through an instrument which tells us to deny that lots of space (exists and) needs be physically travelled between us and our goal.

Interactive distance learning and the Internet comprise inert teaching location. Even interactive distance learning, which technologically dignifies students, should be used sparingly, judiciously, and carefully. We humanize distance learning when we need that technological capability. For teaching on campus and daily learning, even interactive distance learning becomes inert location or inert ideas because teacher and student are physically apart.

Inert ideas as teaching location means that teachers and students are reduced to optics, voice, and anatomic movement. Students perceive data and lights on monitors and computer screens. They and teachers look into cameras and do not make eye contact with a human being present with them. As they talk into microphones, they are not engaging in interpersonal, physical conversation. Their voices are reduced to electronic impulses. Their locations are reduced to physical, geometric, or quantitative areas. Classrooms involve human beings speaking, listening, seeing within the evolving, holistic values of social, immediate existence. The classroom enriches location as interpersonal spaces joined in immediate community.

Lifelong returning to the classroom idea humanizes teaching-learning location. Students spend necessary time and effort to go to the classroom. Their efforts mean rejecting the Internet's and distance learning's false immediacy, where students spend no time travelling to the classroom where the teaching occurs. Student efforts going to the classroom also mean rejecting urban sprawl's requirement of travelling ten, twenty, or more miles to go to the classroom.

Students from Chicago attending Harvard, Stanford, or other school outside Illinois, or Southern Illinois University outside Chicago, would reject two extremes. One extreme involves commuting between Chicago and Cambridge, Massachusetts or Stanford, California each day. The other extreme would be staying home and learning online or going to a distance learning classroom.

The process philosophy of education tells us that learning is a social, interpersonal experience involving students and teachers as human beings. We are not merely optic, otic, and anatomic. Teachers and students are never only perceiving, hearing, and physically moving arms in distance learning or online. They are whole human beings participating in each other's presence. At the other extreme, students are irreducible to bodies which travel long distances in commuting to campuses.

Students are human becomings participating in face-to-face learning. They are never only commuters dependent on speedy vehicles or only neurosensors sitting in front of online computers physically going nowhere.

3. The Commune

Lifelong learning's process philosophy of education tells us to always return to the classroom for our primary location of learning. Classrooms mean students and teachers are physically present with each other. Being physically present does not guarantee good teaching and learning. Physical presence is the necessary social structure for the teacher-student relationship.

Online and interactive distance learning may be needed when students and teachers cannot be physically present and learning must occur. Replacing classrooms with online or interactive distance learning reduces learning location to inert ideas. Classrooms can also be places where no learning occurs.

If students and teachers are together, learning is destroyed when discipline is lax, teachers are authoritarian, students are passive, or the learning situation is otherwise dysfunctional. Students must make the effort to attend class, rejecting long distances to school and relying online or distance learning. In class, teachers and students need dialogue, good physical conditions of heat, light, and so on, and safety.

A process philosophy of lifelong learning tells us to continually maintain a holistic attitude toward the teaching situation. Students and teachers go to class-rooms that are a physically safe, culturally humane, intellectually motivating, and otherwise conducive to learning. Technology, location, interpersonal relations, culture, public safety, good hygienic conditions all constitute the framework for healthy teaching and learning.

I find telling the many efforts of people or ethnic groups to seek statehood. Efforts toward founding states or nations signify that physical location is part of human nature. Human beings need to feel a belonging to the land. They need to feel belonging to a particular place or geographic location. Learning location is no different. The classroom is the place where students come together to learn. Lifelong learning must include the idea that we are always in need of a classroom as the location for most of our teaching and learning. Interactive distance learn-ing and the Internet may have their roles to play. My aim in this chapter is to show that the classroom must repeatedly be the primary location for learning. Replacing classrooms with interactive distance learning reduces to inert ideas.

Four

REHUMANIZING
THE INFORMATION EXPLOSION

Whether we opt for interactive distance learning, the Internet, the classroom, or any combination of these, we need to deal with the information explosion. Inside the distant and traditional classrooms, resimplifying or reorganizing the information explosion is lifelong.

Simplification or reorganization of increasing amounts of data and theory never stops. Simplifying or organizing growing quantities of information means continual resimplification or reorganization of data and theory. We need to always simplify or reorganize the information explosion. Simplification of data and theory is a dynamic, evolving whole. Simplification aims at continually organizing increasing amounts of data and theories into a simple theory or set of theories sufficiently general to explain special theories and data. Allowing the information explosion to be the sum total of increasing data and theory reduces knowledge to inert ideas.

The information explosion is part of the simplification-explosion continuum. Growing amounts of theory and data manifest evolving human beings or becomings. Human beings always need an ongoing, simple, general theory of existence. A simple theory (or set of theories) constantly rehumanizes the growing amounts of theory and data. Rehumanization gives holistic meaning to the information explosion and eliminates outdated data and theory. Human beings are evolving simplifiers who increase theories and data within the holistic context of a more general theory.

I call "inert amounts of information" that increasing quantity of data and special theories which lack theoretical reorganization or resimplification. Inert amounts of information are examples of inert ideas. Inert quantities of information just sit in libraries waiting for holistic frameworks, or elimination if outdated. Resimplification overcomes the inert ideas of exploding amounts of data lacking theory.

1. The Information Explosion

We must learn to continaully resimplify and reorganize the growing quantities of theory and data. A theory or set of theories of existence is irreducible to the information explosion. Relevant amounts must be put into simpler theoretical context.

During the Middle Ages, the Church controlled scholarship. After the Fall of the Middle Ages, inquiry was becoming part of the secular intellectual community not following Church doctrine. Data is due to our assumptions and theories about what data to gather. As scholars collected data and these lead to the evolution of theories, the world experienced the gradual growth of what we now call the information explosion.

Mark Donald Bowles presents an excellent analysis of the historical and philosophical context of the information explosion.[1] He painstakingly points out that the explosion did not start at the end of the Middle Ages. Information and its growth has been the basis of history. Information has always multiplied from pictures on cave walls to the Internet. We need less to fear the increase in the quantity of data and theory, and more to believe in lifelong reorganization and resimplification of information.

If more and more information exists, scholars must specialize and subspecialize with an eye toward overlapping fields and subfields. Specialization and subspecialization are distinct from overspecialization. Specialties and subspecialties give us more and more information about existence. Gaining as much knowledge about the world as possible is not wrong. The failure or refusal of scholars to communicate with each other and to understand how their specialties and subspecialities contribute to the whole of knowledge is wrong. Overspecialization is the lack of communication among scholars and their inability or refusal to see how each specialty and subspecialty is part of all knowledge.

Scholars in subspecialties do wrong when they cannot or will not communicate with others in their own fields. Subspecialists in physics must understand how their subfield relates to the field or specialty of physics, and must communicate with other physicists. These subspecialists should also appreciate the relationship between their subfield and, say, chemistry, theology, and all other disciplines. Overspecialization involves inert ideas in that it rejects the holistic view that specializations and subspecializations relate to each other.

Scholars in the Middle Ages knew most of the knowledge that existed at that time. Twenty-first century scholars know primarily their own subspecialty. If they cannot know all the knowledge that exists, they need not worry about being ignorant. Scholars should know their subspecialty and general isomorphies which underlie two or more subfields and fields.

Human beings do not believe that they should be burdened with vast quantities of data and theories. Alfred North Whitehead would call such burdening as inert ideas in terms of inert quantities of data. Scholars seek theories to simplify or explain vast amounts of data, and general theory or theories to simplify or explain vast amounts of theories and data. I add that scholars seek a general theory to explain numerically nonthreatening (two or more, never vast amounts of) theories.

2. Simplifying Data Explosion

Lifelong simplifying of data involves continual development of a theory or few general theories to explain the growing quantity of data. Alfred North Whitehead did not have the information overload of the Twenty-First century. The amount of data he saw was sufficient to have him warn us about increasing information.

Alfred North Whitehead says the university must emphasize generality and not a collection of data.[2] General principles give perspective and context to increasing quantities of data. Simplifying and organizing the large quantities of data means that theory helps us see a whole underlying the vast amounts of information. A simplifying theory's holistic view enables us to reject the notion that each piece of increasing quantities of data stands alone and must be considered without a relationship to other data.

As we gain more and more data, we must continually seek a more general, simpler theory to explain the most current increases in the quantity of facts. If the smallest amount of information does not explain itself or comprise a theory or principle, larger quantities are not the context in which data makes sense. Theory is irreducible to data, and to the exploding quantities of data.

A theory simplifying increasing amounts of data explains this growing quantity of information. This theory also accomplishes another task. A simplifying theory which enables us to retain relevant data, helps us get rid of irrelevant data. Some emerging data is relevant and the remainder is irrelevant. Some currently relevant informtion will become obsolete later and will have to be jettisoned when it becomes outdated.

Getting rid of obsolete data is part of a bigger, more general idea of society. Alfred North Whitehead speaks about the need to continually prune excess symbols.[3] Society manifests itself through symbols. These symbols may be religious, intellectual, cultural, governmental, organizational, and so on. We can have excess buildings, spaces in existing buildings, processes, organizational procedures, and so on. Bureaucracy is an example of the need for pruning. Multiculturalism exemplifies a trend of cultures and ethnic groups seeking their own identities in the midst of the need for unity.

In time every civilization develops symbols in quantities which can overwhelm people. Inert ideas in terms of excess or dangerous amounts of symbolism is always possible, and should continually be simplified or eliminated.

Information is a symbol and excess quantities can overwhelm us. We need to continually rethink the meaning and relevance of increasing amounts of data. Rethinking involves articulating new theories and modifying existing theories to explain larger and larger amounts of information, and jettison obsolete material. A university's role is to shed data in favor of theories.[4]

We may speak of the downsizing of the explosion of data. Downsizing denotes quantitative lessening. If we start with downsizing of knowledge instead of reorganizing data in terms of values and theoretical orientation, we may eliminate relevant data. Downsizing must be in light of lifelong adherence to basic theory allowing us to cut back on the amount of data. Ockham's Razor is the philosophical idea that we must never assume more symbols than we need for explanations. I argue that the assumption involves values orienting using a razor to cut needless symbols. Elimination must be based on values and orientation. We should not allow elimination to be our starting point. We jettison excess data not because we have nothing else to do and want to do something. We jettison excess data only in light of a simpler, underlying idea indicating which data is valuable. Scholars must start with developing values and a holistic vision, and not by wondering what to eliminate. Developing the holistic context will lead to what is not holistic and what ought be taken away.

By jettisoning obsolete data I do not mean repression. As research develops, we see the irrelevance of some existing data. We must replace outdated material with newer information. For example, the Copernican Revolution told us that the earth revolves around the sun. Copernican cosmology replaces Ptolemaic cosmology that the sun revolves around the earth. By eliminating outdated or irrelevant data, I do not mean getting rid of existing information which does not appeal currently to scholars. My point is only that once we find data that shows previous data incorrect, we correct our perspectives.

Richard E. Bellman talks about simplifying increasing amounts of data and theory.[5] His focus is on mathematics, but he extends his ideas to all scholars. Mathematicians, as other scholars, see knowledge as more than the exponentially growing amounts of facts. Mathematicians seek structures or theories that will simplify vast amounts of data in their field.[6] An explosion of information is never sufficient for any field of knowledge. Richard E. Bellman would concur that the search for theory explaining growing quantities of data is lifelong. Accepting vast amounts of data without theory means reducing the quantity to inert ideas.

By search, Richard E. Bellman is not implying that we first collect large amounts of data and then seek theory. We start with a theory which explains existing quantities of data. As data increases, we modify the existing theory or seek to expand and renew the theory. We cannot understand mathematics without theories putting increasing quantities of quantitative thinking into holistic, qualitative perspective. Mathematicians are to continually develop theories to explain exponentially growing data in their field. Let me turn to the field of law in which a professional warns against reducible the subject-matter to quantities of data.

James Doherty concurs that growing amounts of data is meaningless without underlying principles.[7] He is an assistant public defender and warns trial lawyers about how to present their cases. Whether they prosecute or defend, they must cite cases supporting their view. Trial lawyers should cite cases involving principles and never those that are wordy. Principles and not verbiage is controlling. Legal meaning is always found in principles and not how much a lawyer talks or says. Quality of information underlies quantity of information. Lawyers win cases not by how much information they present or how long they talk, but by what they say and how they say it.

The exploding quantities of information devoid of theory are inert quantities. Our goal should be living or theoretically oriented amounts of data. Theory and not excess data provides knowledge. If teachers may not pack the smallest amount of data into student's minds as though articles in a trunk, instructors should not pack larger quantities into the brain. The more general theory enables us to give meaning to growing amounts of relevant data, and eliminate outdated material. From the perspective of Alfred North Whitehead, a university's role is the lifelong development of a simple apparatus[8] or principle with the widest possible application for data. In light of the information explosion, the university's responsibility become more complex. The university's duty must be the lifelong articulation of simplifying theories with the widest possible application for exponentially growing quantities of information. If the smallest quantity of data can be a burden on the memory, exploding amounts are even greater headaches and serious problems including the disorganization of data. From the perspective of Alfred North Whitehead, fools reject data, and pedants dislike theory.[9] Carrying that idea forward, the ultimate pedant collects as much data as possible and expects the larger quantity to explain the world.

3. Simplifying the Explosion of Theory

I noted James J. Doherty's point that principles are controling and verbiage is meaningless. Principles are synonymous with theories. Principles or theories are partly sufficient for meaning. Principles or theories explain and simplify large amounts of data. In time, exploding amounts of principles require more general and simpler principles or theories. Theory should be defined as giving meaning to or simplifying growing amounts of data. In addition, theory must be defined as providing simplification or holistic context for growing quantities of less general theories.

When we speak of data needing theory we imply that any amount of theories is sufficient. From this perspective, the more theories we articulate to simplify exploding amounts of data, the better. Each simplifying theory stands. Thousands of simplifying theories are justified because they are theories. This perspective implies that an overwhelming number of theories is good because each explains a set of data. The implication derives from the definition of theory as that which explains data. Presumably, if theory explains data, any number of theories is satisfactory because they explain data. Increasing number of theories need fewer general theories. The truth is we need a more complex definition of theory.

Richard E. Bellman says when theories increase and threaten to overwhelm us, we need simpler theory.[10] A general theory is required to prune, clarify, and explain existing theories. From the perspective of Richard E. Bellman, increasing quantities of theories constitute more and more subspecialties within existing specialties. More subspecialties pose a danger to intellectuals. The increasing number of subspecialties can result in fragmentation within disciplines and the inability of inter- and intradisciplinary communication.

If overwhelming amounts of data require theory, larger quantities of theory similarly need a more general, simpler theory for a holistic view of vast amounts of data and theory. The more general theory or set of theories simplifies less general theories. Less general theories are justified, and require a theory of theories for meaningfulness. Less general or more specialized theories reflect reality but require the more general and less specific theories in order to comprise holistic reality. Theory as well as data increases in amount. To restate James J. Doherty, theory verbiage is as meaningless as data verbiage, and needs simpler theory to eliminate or replace overwhelming amounts of theory. More and more theories providing holistic context to data are insufficient. Excess quantities of theories devoid of a more general theory can create intellectual fragmentation. Verbiage of theories is meaningless; simpler theory or set of theories underlying less general theories provide controlling wholeness.

Scholars in all specialties and subspecialties must deal with efforts toward resimplification or reorganization of information. In anthropology, scholars are seriously concerned with the information explosion's impact on compartmentalization and fragmentation. Subfields are emerging like topsy, including biological and archaeological anthropology. The emergence of subspecialties or subfields is not inherently bad. They tell us more about humanity.

Anthropologists Mariam Rodin, Karen Michaelsen, and Michael Britan are anxious about the subfields causing communication breakdown among anthropologists, and secondly, between anthropologists and other fields.[11] Social, biological, and archaeological anthropologists are unable to communicate with each other due to fragmented terminologies and compartmentalized concepts. More broadly, anthropologists must work together with engineers, geneticists, planners, managers, computer scientists, and others. Many anthropologists believe that the application of system theory provides the solution to bringing about communication within anthropology and among anthropologists and other disciplines.[12] System theory overcomes the inert ideas that anthropological subspecialists need not communicate with each other or with specialists in other fields.

System theory and the idea of isomorphies underlying disciplines can comprise the most basic role of the liberal arts: to relate disciplines. From the perspective of the information explosion, system theory relates disciplines and subdisciplines by facilitating relationships among newer theories and more data within disciplines. Ideas including equilibrium, energy, and the relation between parts and wholes, are some homologies. Systems thinking means that we approach a subject with divergent aspects as a whole. We need to see the total picture and never isolate parts from the holistic context. Homologies can help us develop theories simplifying data and special theories.

Anthropologist, John M. Van Deusen[13] argues that the information explosion must be slowed down. He maintains that we must now spend time developing simple concepts encompassing masses of theories and data. The time has come to emphasize simplicity over the generation and distribution of information. His ideas, while holistic, require caution about the need for simplicity in the information explosion.

Reality and information are a process. We cannot and should not now or at any time cease research and the growth of information. Theories and data are necessary for us to learn about existence. We cannot divide history into a time for research and development of data and theory, and a time for simplifying the information explosion. Research adds to the quantity of information. The role of research is to contribute to the amount of data and theory in an organized, holistic, evolutionary fashion. Growing amounts of data and theory give us a better picture of realty's complex nature. Refining our classifications and organization of data and theory helps provide the holistic, dynamic framework in which to view that increase of information.

Dividing time into times for developing specialization and subspecialization, and for unifying knowledge, presents a serious problem. How long do we do research to develop specialties and subspecialties, and then to develop unifying principles? Do we spend months and years on disciplinarity and then succeeding months or years on interdisciplinarity? Such temporal division is impractical and unreasonable. Scholars cannot determine how much time any kind of research must take. The better alternative is to ask disciplinarians do their research, and others who prefer strictly interdisciplinary work do their job.

Taking serendipity into account, we cannot say that the growth of information is inherently bad. Biologists, chemists, theologians, and others can do disciplinary research. In the process, many will find and contribute interdisciplinary theories. Scholars such as those with the International Society for Systems Science (ISSS) can continually do interdisciplinary work with resimplification. Disciplinary work gives us generally more insight into special data and theories, and interdisciplinary efforts insight into more general ideas and values. Disciplinarity need not inherently mean more data and theory in the divisive sense. Disciplinarity and subspecialized information can contribute toward overlapping ideas.

When the number of theories and subdisciplines explode, isomorphies contribute a wholeness by simplifying structures underlying previously unrelated, overwhelming quantities of subspecialties. The ISSS provides homologies or isomorphies common to two or more separate fields. These fields can then become one, or see themselves as commonly rooted. Homologies enable scholars to see overlaps, connections, or interrelating among two or more disciplines or subdisciplines, specialties or subspecialties.

Simplification must be as lifelong as growth. Simplification is different from oversimplification. Simplification produces a unifying, holistic framework in which to view or understand complexity and diversity. Holistic frameworks do not aim at rejecting complexity or diversity. The aim of simplification is to develop an intelligible whole in which multiplicity makes sense. Oversimplification denies the validity of diversity or complexity, and sees the world as a naive, undifferentiated whole devoid of complexity. Substitute specialization or subspecialization for complexity, diversity, and multiplicity. Substitution allows us to see that simplification accepts and puts specialties and subspecialties into a coherent whole, while oversimplification denies the validity of those specialities and subspecialties.

Scholars can and should always do research. Books and articles in specialized and subspecialized fields can unintentionally provide evidence or support for simplicity. Some scholars can, if they prefer, do specialized research. Others, if they so like, can do interdisciplinary writing. The growth and dissemination of information does not inherently cause chaos.

Readers may ask how I can defend specialization, subspecialization, and resimplification at the same time. If we must always resimplify, should we allow some scholars to specialize and subspecialize without much thought to resimplification? My view is that scholars in one field or subfield must be allowed to generate specialized and subspecialized information as long as they acknowledge their contributions within holistic or interdisciplinary contexts. Each contribution toward specialized and subspecialized growth must take into account how this relates to the bigger picture of knowledge. Scholars should never do specialized and subspecialized research as though their fields and subfields exist alone, and their information unrelated to all knowledge. As an example, consider biology, anthropology, and chemistry expanding their information while relating to each other and other fields. Specialists and subspecialists acknowledge unity as they periodically return to school to rethink the holistic context of their fields and subfields.

Outside anthropology, biology and chemistry have numerous subspecialties, sub-subspecialties, and so on. Each sub and sub-subspecialty still has to communicate with the specialty. Biology subspecialists, sub-subspecialists, and further subspecialists continue to be biologists. Chemistry subspecialists, sub-subspecialists, and further subspecialists are still chemists.

The information explosion has created infinite subspecializations since the 1600s. When our disciplines were created, scholars were able to understand all aspects of knowledge. They were biologists, mathematicians, and so on. The information explosion has changed that dramatically. What the explosion has not changed is that the farthest level of subspecialization within a field continues to be a member identified within that general discipline.

Manfred Clynes argues against allowing the information explosion to dictate a fragmentation of human nature.[14] The development of science, for example, has given us unrelated approaches in psychology, anatomy, biochemistry, physiology, and biophysics. The result is the *psychological* person, the *anatomic* person, the *biochemical* perspective, and so on. Manfred Clynes maintains that the functioning human being is an evolving whole instead of fragmented parts.

We are not physiological, *and* anatomic, *and* biochemical. Human beings are physiological-biochemical-and-so-on. The holistic view involves fundamental unity and not the juxtaposition of inherently diverse, unrelated parts. Manfred Clynes sees hope in the integrative field of biocybernetics. He finds that biocybernetics can offer an holistic alternative to the fragmentation brought about by the information explosion in the sciences.

Biocybernetics is not currently the trend or buzz word in interdisciplinary thinking. My point is that Manfred Clynes argues that reality is one and not fragmented. Reality is not trees, and mountains, and water. Reality is a whole of trees, mountains, and water integrally related. Knowledge is not physics and chemistry, and religion. Reality is a a physical-chemical-religious-etc. unity.

Russell L. Ackoff says nature is not organized in the way that universities are compartmentalized.[15] He would say that nature is not subdepartmentalized as are our university departments and disciplines. Disciplines need lifelong vigilance against intra departmental as well as interdepartmental fragmentation.

Psychologists are doing disciplinary work in terms of interdisciplinary orientations. Lisa Rabasca[16] tells of plans by Walter Mischel to develop conceptual integration among psychological subfields, and psychology and other disciplines. Walter Mischel dislikes the idea of a field becoming a psychological science in its own right only to split from psychology and generate isolated ideas. Subdisciplines emerge and existing disciplines see themselves as having clear-cut boundaries primarily for political and history instead of natural reasons.

When specialties and subspecialties emerge for natural reasons, cross-fertilization is the answer for unity. George Waltz[17] interviews Vannevar Bush concerning the growing amounts of subspecialties. Vannevar Bush notes that we will have more and more subspecialties coupled with increasing cross-fertilization among the subfields. Vannevar Bush corrects the connotation of scholars who suggest that we stop or slow down the explosion of information and replace it with generalized concepts. We need not slow down anything. Increasing subspecialization reveals the multifaceted nature of existence. As each subspecialty unfolds, we understand and appreciate more of reality. Each subfield, in turn, must be seen within the larger context of a discipline or field. No subspecialty stands alone and represents an isolated reality.

Some scholars do research and increase subspecialization and specialization. Other scholars, such as those in homological research, provide us with interdisciplinary and intradisciplinary isomorphies. We should make no mistake about scholars who do non-homological research. Biologists, psychologists, philosophers, historians, and other not directly involved in researching isomorphies, can and do, in the course of their work, find isomorphies even if these are serendipitous.

Simplifying the information explosion through reorganization of knowledge reminds me of religion. Hindus believe in much myth and ritual. The Buddha reacts against ritualism and says we need to eliminate the idea of ritual. Ironically, Buddhism is not monolithic. Mahayana Buddhism is highly ritualistic, and Hinayana Buddhism eschews ritual. I argue that we need to see that increases in ritual are not necessarily bad, and that an implosion of ritual not inherently good. Hindu ritualism expresses polytheism, and Buddha brings in a nontheism. Simplification should not mean oversimplification. Simplification in religion can mean a periodic return to a monotheism. We would look toward a single God for all things instead of needing to recall the name of the particular god appropriate for a certain circumstance.

Intellectually or cognitively, the growing amount of theories and data do not need to be eliminated. We can retain, reorganize, and resimplify these quantities in terms of a more general theory of theories. Do I mean that in religion we need a God of gods? I do not see the need for a God of special gods. Religions can have a God of the Prophets and great persons of spirituality. Cognitively and spiritually, a general context of special contexts evolves toward a taxonomy of taxonomies. A general theory explains special theories and data, a God expresses power through specific people, prophets, and so on.

If holy people (prophets, etc.) proliferate, we do not eliminate them. The holy people are to be within the context of the Holy. If many gods, heroes, etc., exist, we must treat them by seeing them as holies within the larger, Holy context of a God. The holy people by themselves constitute fragmentation of holiness and possible polytheism. Taking them away can result in non- or a-theism: the opposite of the holy or whole. Intellectually, proliferating wholes and data does not mean we stop producing the wholes. We must seek the most general whole of wholes. Specific wholes without the general whole comprise compartmentalization and fragmentation: the cognitive or intellectual parallel to polytheism. A lack of wholes and data comprise an a-cognition or anti-intellectualism: the academic parallel to atheism.

The Old English *hale* is the root of holiness and wholeness.[18] Holiness means wholeness, and wholeness is reflected in the sacred as holiness. The holy is an irreducible whole; wholeness characterizes an irreducible holiness. A theology of culture finds the holy or whole amid parts of culture and knowledge, and can lead toward foundations of interdisciplinary. Once we discern the holy or sacred amid a variety of items including the arts, sciences, or arts and sciences, we are on the road toward unifying knowledge and reaching interdisciplinary. I have written about this in researching the connection between religion and interdisciplinarity.[19]

Getting rid of irrelevant theories is as crucial as eliminating outdated data. I repeat the idea of replacing geocentric with heliocentric cosmology. We need not eliminate theories which are currently irrelevant or unfashionable. I argue that once the arts or sciences discover a theory that better explains data, we then consider discarding the outdated theory.

Vast amounts of theory lacking a more general theory of theories becomes inert ideas. We can prevent inert ideas of theory by seeking a general theory underlying special and vast amounts of intradisciplinary general theories.

I need to make another point about simplifying the information explosion. That point concerns the simplification of a nonthreatening number of theories emerging from the threatening quantities of data.

4. Simplifying Nonexploding Theories

Richard E. Bellman says above that we need a theory to simply overwhelming quantities of data, and a general, simpler theory to simply threatening amounts of theories. If data can increase exponentially, so can theories. My position is that a third perspective enters in.

The exploding amount of data can result in a few theories which are fragmented and unrelated. Overwhelming quantities of data do not necessarily always result in overwhelming quantities of theories. When the increase in data is shockingly large, the result can be a nonexploding multiplicity of theories. The result is not that we have excess amounts of theory as in my previous section. The problems becomes fragmentation. Two, three, or more theories explaining similar phenomena are not a lot of theories. The two, three, or more theories comprise a numerically, quantitatively few or simple multiplicity or plurality of theories. Even this small amount of theories explaining common reality must be simplified into one, unifying theory. A common reality is always one reality, one existence. One reality requires one theory and never two or more, or any numerically small number of theories. The need for simplifying a nonthreatening, nonexploding number of theories resulting from the explosion of data, is lifelong.

The few theories attempting to explain a single reality constitute fragmentation or inert ideas. They are unrelated to each and make us think that a single reality has two or more distinct aspects to it. Vast amounts of theories, like exploding quantities of data, are a burden on the memory. Two, three, or more but not an overwhelming number of theories can be kept in mind. The problem these pose is a logical one. We can memorize a few theories but believe that logically reality is one, and a single reality requires a unifying theory.

Physics is a case in point. Albert Einstein saw physical reality and attempted to integrate relativity and quantum theories. He developed relativity theory to explain large masses in space, Werner Heisenberg developed an opposing, quantum theory explaining the microscopic and submicroscopic universe. The physical universe is one. Einstein and others attempt to show that one unifying field theory can explain very large and very small physical reality. The physical universe does not consist of large masses (stars, planets, comets, etc.) *and* small or microcosmic, atomic and subatomic particles. Physical reality comprises a single unity of the large and small. A single, unifying, simplifying field theory would demonstrate that the macrocosmic and microcosmic exist as an integral whole.

I turn from the quantitative world of physics to the qualitative milieu of mythology. Julian Pitt-Rivers notes that Paul Ricoeur and Claude Lévi-Strauss are trying to determine a general theory of mythology.[20] Paul Ricoeur believes in a single theory of mythology because myth is a single reality; Claude Lévi-Strauss says pure and edited myths each need different theories. From the perspective of Julian-Pitt Rivers, Claude Lévi-Strauss ignores the point that myth emerges from ever changing culture.[21] Mythologies are edited as soon as they are developed. Modification, interpretation, and evolution of myth occurs all the time. Every myth is a process being continually reinterpreted. From efforts toward a unified view of mythology, I speak of efforts to unify aspects of law.

Jerome Hall argues that we currently have many theories of criminal law, and that our challenge must be the lifelong search for a universal theory of criminal law.[22] A unifying theory of criminal law would replace existing multiplicities of such theories and help orient empirical research toward a general theory. Jerome

Hall says that all our research, data, and theories are not yet helping us answer questions about punishment, deterance, rehabilitation, procedure, and so on. Let me now point out an endeavor for unity in biology.

In the field of biology, scholars find a plurality or theories of bioenergy and say that biologists must develop a single, unifying theory of how living organisms use energy. Energy in living organisms is a single concept and requires a simple theory.[23] Scholars who want to discern a single theory of bioenergetics are saying that energy in living creatures does not exist in two or more states or existences. Biological energy is one process or reality. Let me turn from the world of academia to the practical world of safety in the community.

Lots of information exists about fire safety, architecture, arson, law enforcement, and related issues concerning fire codes. The large quantities of data concerning fire safety, and so on, has produced two, and sometimes more, fire codes for the nation. Some professionals believe that fire safety is a single theme and we must have a single code instead of two or more codes.[24] Different states in the nation cannot abide by different rules. Such differentiation would require architects, executives, fire officials, and everyone to always think of a state's rule and not a national code.

The problem of nonthreatening number of theories produced by a threatening number of data is as necessary to resolve as the problem of threatening quantities of theories. Overwhelming quantities of theories must be put into simplified perspective so we may understand the total, evolving picture without resorting to vast amounts of explanations. Nonoverwhelming amounts of theories need simpler theory so that we may be better communication instead of fragmentation manifesting a single reality. Threatening amounts of data and subtheories result in numerically nonthreatening multiplicity of theories constituting the burden of fragmentation. The burden of fragmentation created by a small number of unrelated theories explaining the same thing is as crucial to solve as the burden of memorizing vast amounts of theories.

A simpler, general theory for nonthreatening and threatening quantities of theory and data poses an intriguing issue. We are to simplify vast amounts and even small numbers of theories because reality is one. Consider what I have said. Physical reality requires a theory to unify relativity and quantum theories. Mythological reality needs a single theory of mythology. Legal processes are one and need a universal theory of criminal law. Each of these realities comprise reality, existence, or human beings. If we should not have inert ideas or fragmentation among specific theories in given fields, we should not have inert ideas or fragmentation among the totality of unifying theories.

My next section considers a general theory of theories. A general theory of theories comprises a basic taxonomy or fundamental whole giving meaning and context to all special wholes. Such a general theory provides the wholness whereby the specific theories can be related to each other. When researchers find specific theiries these investigators wish to know the more fundamental idea underlying the particular theories.

5. General Theory of Theories

By a general theory of theories I mean a general taxonomy of all special theories. If physical theories must be unified, if we need a general theory of mythology, if a general theory of criminal law is required, what of a general theory of existence? My present work is a modest effort toward a general theory simplifying all theories. I argue for a general theory, without going into detail about its complexities. My effort is to say that we need a general taxonomy (liberal arts) homologically underlying special taxonomies (the disciplines including arts and sciences). That general taxonomy involves the various kinds of lifelong learning as pointed out in my chapters. The general taxonomy is distilled from and takes into account the information explosion.

Alfred North Whitehead says philosophy is the critique of abstractions.[25] We need to think, and he says we cannot think without abstractions. Abstractions can mean the small amount data. They can also be the development of large quantities of data, of theories, and of small quantities of theories requiring even fewer general, more simplied theories. Philosophy as critique of increasing amounts of abstractions involves disclosing the holistic foundations of exploding amounts of data and theories, and multiple theories in the same field. Philosophy becomes the holistic approach to exploding amounts of knowledge.

Library science and the organization of knowledge becomes fundamental to lifelong simplicity of the information explosion. Philosophy as the critique of large amounts of data and theory abstractions, can be coupled with library science. Philosophers can collaborate with librarians to organize all material into homologies comprising a liberal arts section, and into disciplinary homologies constituting a section for the various arts and sciences.

6. Unchecked Explosion

What happens if we never simplify the information? Data would overwhelm us without a simplifying theory. What happens with overwhelming theories? Too many theories would similarly threaten our cognitive abilities. A few unifying theories in most fields would be logically bothersome since each theory in a given field is another way of explaining the same phenomena. Two different theories for the same phenomena are one too many theories.

I do not mean that a field, for example biology, must have only one of two or more existing theories, whatever the circumstance. When two or more theories exist in a given discipline, such as relativity and quantum theories physics, we need to try to find a common, more general theory to incorporate and integrate these competing theories. I do not suggest that seeing multiple theories, we automatically get rid of one of them. We may eventually not eliminate either one. Both theories may continue to exist as particular manifestations of a larger, more simplified or general framework. In physics, a unified field theory would not eliminate quantum and relativity theories. A unifying field theory in physics would only provide a larger context for seeing that relativity and quantum ideas are basically differing aspects of a single concept.

An explosion of data without theoretical context has no meaning. Increasing quantities of data and theory lacking ongoing resimplification become inert information. We must have meaning and direction. A problem in the government is that its intelligence agencies may have overwhelming amounts of data about other countries, but no orienting theory about foreign affairs.[26] Unless governments know what to do in foreign affairs, the biggest intelligence agencies are of no use. The intelligence agencies' information is only inert data. A society and its government must decide on how they will deal with foreign countries. That decision requires information, but the information will be part of an overall philosophy of foreign affairs.

A central issue in governmental intelligence is whether to listen in on a friendly, and often unfriendly nation's communications. Should we have an intelligence agency? Whether we bug foreign governments does not depend on any information we have on them. Listening in secret depends on our philosophy, values, ideas, and beliefs about life, foreign affairs, and communications. What we do with the information we gather also depends on our values and not the amount of data we collect.

Harry Howe Ransom warns[27] that successful foreign affairs depends much less on the quantity of data stored in our intelligence libraries and more in the theoretical orientations giving us direction and purpose to that data for international affairs. Lots of data does mean national security. How we use, classify, and interpret that data comprises security.

The issue of quantity threatens academe. Lots of data and lots of intradisciplinary theories do not comprise a good library.[28] A library full of the latest books and periodicals can have poor security and lose valuable material. Students and professors without values do not have the capability to use information. The students and professors need theoretical and ethical purpose to use the scholarly material.

James Hall, mentioned above, notes that empirical research and information in criminal law does not insure improving our knowledge of crime, justice, punishment, and the entire host of questions in criminal law. We need orientation contexts to guide and direct the information explosion. Only a developing context can bring about a holistic framework for relevant data and theories, and help us prune irrelevant information.

I am reminded of nuclear physics and the contemporary method of imploding large buildings with dynamite. I am not justifying nuclear reactors. My point is that atomic and hydrogen bombs manifest uncontrolled nuclear explosions. Why we build and explode them manifest our philosophy and values of national security, weapons, and world affairs. Nations build nuclear weapons because they believe that such weapons are necessary. Nuclear reactors depend on society's belief that these are necessary for energy. Nuclear reactors represent controlled nuclear reaction. The use of dynamiting buildings is another example of controlling explosions. We dynamite buildings by carefully calculating the amount and placement of dynamite so that the explosions bring down a building without hurting or killing people and without damaging nearby buildings.

Controlling the information explosion is necessary. Without theoretical and value foundations, increasing quantities of data and theories mean nothing. We need a general framework for understanding the data and theories, and for helping eliminate irrelevant data and theories. Elimination of irrelevant data and theory must be done with caution. I do not suggest that we get rid of ideas and information which many thinkers consider wrong. Today's wrong ideas may be tomorrow's truth. By getting rid of irrelevant information I mean only that once we replace an existing data or theory with a newer theory or set of theories which best explain realty, we can then get rid of the outdated material.

7. Overcontrolling the Explosion

Checking the information explosion is lifelong. We cannot allow data and theories to overwhelm us cognitively or logically. The same can be said in reverse.

Theory is aimed at simplifying existing data in the smallest amounts. Simplifying the smallest quantity of data requires data. Theory and data are continuous. To oversimplify existing data is self-defeating because theory has to explain data. Theory is also aimed at simplifying or explaining exploding quantities of data. Simplifying exploding amounts of data requires vast amounts of data to be explained. Theory and vast quantities of data are continuous. To oversimplify large quantities of data is wrong because theory has to explain vast amounts of data. Similarly, simplifying or explaining multiple and exploding amounts of theories requires those pluralistic and exploding amounts of theories. A general theory is continuous with subtheories to be explained. If data and theories are to be jettisoned, the pruning must be cautious and comes later so as not to compel a dangerous parsimony.

Rarified theories unable to explain the world comprise a theoretical solipsism.[29] Theories explain the world of experience. Too parsimonious a theory or set of theories become detached from the real world and explain nothing. The theory-data continuum, theory-exploding data continuum, general theory-plural theories continuum, and the general theory-exploding theories continuum must all be taken seriously. Vast amounts of data need respect and analysis instead of oversimplification. Multiple and exploding amounts of theories must be taken into account and not quickly dismissed as unnecessary.

8. Conclusion

Simplicity, reorganization, or parsimony is a lifelong juggling act. We need to understand that lifelong learning and theorizing are to be done within the real world. Lifelong learning is the effort to see how we can deal effectively with changes in the world. Ongoing education is never the attempt to dismiss the world or see how we may do without experience. Constantly relating to the world is a problem which John VanDeusen can have if he separated history or time into a time for growth and dissemination of data and a time for parsimony. Parsimony without ongoing growth of information can fall into the trap of oversimplification.

Readers may be saying the trap is impossible due to the existing volume of overwhelming information. My reply is that if we stop growth or suggest that growth slow down, we become dangerously close to saying that parsimony and theory are our only task at that time. Our scholarly task is the lifelong relating of simplicity to ongoing rush of data and theory.

Some scholars can contribute specialized research with the growth and dissemination of information as long as this does not curtail unity and lead to departmentalization. Other scholars can have a new specialty: unity or simplification. Philosophers and philosophers of education, including myself, fit into the new specialty. They would simplify the information explosion without asking their colleagues to stop developing data.

My task, our task, would be to articulate the foundations of the liberal arts. In so doing, we develop the directions and reveal values for specialization and subspecialization. The philosophical role in the information explosion is to bring forth a theoretical framework comprising direction for increasing amounts of data and theory in general education and specialization.

A process philosophy of education shows that philosophy and education can combine with library science in the lifelong effort to provide meaningful information to students and professors. The library is the institution or university department directly and primarily concerning with knowledge. By definition and default, the library is the one nondepartmental, interdepartmental, or transdepartmental department. Librarians work, like it or not, with all specialists and subspecialists from all specialties.

To the extent that philosophy is the critique of increasing amounts of data and theory abstractions, philosophers have a tremendous duty. They should encourage educators and library science professionals toward lifelong integration of the wholes and values underlying general and specialized learning. Such integration comprises ongoing theoretical simplification and clarification for the information explosion.

Huston C. Smith[30] remarks that our university libraries, and presumably other libraries, must continually seek simplifying, holistic theory and not just vast amounts of data and special theories. Books, periodicals, and in the Internet age, audio-visual and other electronic media, reflect underlying assumptions and contexts that we must always modify in light of research. Values exist and are irreducible to the vast quantities of information on library shelves or on disc. Wholeness and values are the requirements for a healthy society which gains more knowledge and always needs the context in which data is meaningful.

Wholeness and values are fundamental to life and thought even if we do not sense their presence. Kenneth E. Boulding writes a brilliant work, *The Image*,[31] revealing the reality of wholeness throughout much of knowledge. Our disciplines and subdisciplines are based on theoretical and value-laden judgments and assumptions whether we realize this or not. Any writing sitting on the library shelf consists of the holistic perspective even if authors deny the reality of wholeness. Authors' views color or orient their works. Authors who acknowledge the existence of wholeness and values are being honest. Those who reject the idea that their values orient or color their thoughts are being dishonest.

I argue that a taxonomy of taxonomies is a whole of a set of wholes or values including the chapters of my present book. Fundamental to any evolving knowledge is the notion of lifelong learning and its subsets of lifelong academic work: we must always humanize distance learning, learning location, information explosion, specialized study, specialized motions, and data.

Within the general context of all aspects of lifelong learning, we can begin to carefully categorize and classify the arts and sciences. As with all things, my categories or chapter headings are not written in stone. They evolve. I am prepared, as is David G. Barnum who I mentioned in chapter one, to have readers think about my ideas in terms of ongoing analysis. I argue that the information explosion should continue to provide increasing theories and data about existence. Authors have the duty to publish, and allow and adjust to criticism. Readers who do not author, and authors have the right and duty to engage in dialogue with each other, and direct authors to rethink positions. The information explosion is not basically a threat. Increasing information is another opportunity whereby lifelong education rehumanizes work, academia, and society. Resimplification of the information explosion prevents inert ideas in terms of vast amounts of data, theory, and even of a few fragmented theories.

Five

REHUMANIZING DISCIPLINARITY

Inside simplifying the information explosion, liberal arts is lifelong. Resimplification or reorganization of the growing amount of data and theory reveals general education giving value and humanization to specialization. General education does not stop after college. Workers returning to study must always restudy liberal arts. General education is a dynamic, evolving process continuing throughout life. I can argue that liberal arts is necessary for college students. I need to argue for liberal arts as the basis for specialized study after college and graduate school.

Specialized study is part of ongoing learning. Even if workers return to school throughout life, studying their specialization is insufficient because specialties lacking general education comprise inert ideas. Learning is irreducible to the sum of exploding amounts of data and theory. People must always learn liberating values and wholes underlying specialization.

My present chapter argues that students are irreducible to studying specialization throughout life without general education. They are fundamentally whole human beings expressing their evolving nature through everchanging disciplinary boundaries and job situations. Liberal arts humanize specialized study. Evolving, generalist human beings always study liberal arts. Studying only specialization each time workers return to school reduces specialized study to inert disciplinarity.

1. Liberal Arts Never End

Workers return to school to relearn about their jobs. Similarly liberal arts is here to stay and indispensable. Liberal arts is lifelong as is the study of specialization. Workers return to school to relearn specialization. They return also to relearn general education as the holistic foundations of specialized study. My previous chapter speaks about ongoing resimplification, values, and holistic reorganization of the information explosion. My present chapter looks at the reorganization as the ongoing liberal arts giving holistic meaning and values underlying specialized and subspecialized study.

Henry Winthrop writes that liberal arts and science must be learned throughout life and not restricted to college.[1] Students in graduate school and beyond must always return to study the liberal arts as an ongoing foundation for 'specialization'. If students should learn liberal arts and sciences during college, they ought to continue studying general education after their college years. Liberal arts should be part of graduate and undergraduate studies. Learning about wholeness and values does not stop after college. Studying the holistic approach does not cease after graduate school. Specialized study requires the holistic orientations and values of liberal arts and sciences throughout lifelong learning.

Paul Dressel[2] indicates that learning the liberal arts only in the undergraduate years presents a problem. The traditional system forcing students to complete general education during the college years concerns the issue of cramming all the liberal arts into a given time. Students are forced to cover too much material in too short a time when compelled to start and conclude general education as undergraduates. If we restrict liberal arts to college, we are painting ourselves into the corner. The material we select takes time to learn, to sink in, to be related to other material. We can select only so much material to teach in a short amount of time.

We are wrong to believe that liberal arts comprises a limited number of ideas and requires little time for studying and appreciating those ideas. Lifelong learning tells us to expand our horizons. The college years should provide an introduction to specialization and to liberal arts. College should introduce and not complete liberal arts. Lifelong learning says that college and even graduate school cannot complete liberal arts. General education is lifelong and requires continual return to the academic world for restudy.

Two years of general education can never exhaust the material which students must cover. General education is never exhausted. The traditional system suggests that the two year sequence of material is all that constitutes general education.

To restrict general education to college is to say that liberal arts is a static, unchanging content. The static notion of liberal arts reduces general education to inert ideas. General education is a process of ongoing perspective. The more we restrict liberal arts to college, the greater the problem of what we are to teach as general education. With only the college years as our parameter, our selection is limited. Lifelog learning solves that problem. We introduce students to liberal arts during college, and can reintroduce them throughout life to what they just learned. We can and must introduce and reintroduce them to more material throughout life.

Exposure to life can become as asset to learning. Paul Dressel says that only a continual effort can provide the opportunities for students to effectively learn the evolving, holistic values of liberal arts.[3] Lifelong learning as a process philosophy of education allows students to acquire, incubate, and gradually assimilate general education's interdisciplinary vision. The effort to learn general education cannot stop in college. As students graduate and enter the workforce, they are also growing as adults in the real world. Daily life affords the chances to see and experience more of existence. Work alternating with school enable students to continually mature in their rethinking of the liberating arts.

Students in their early twenties are not necessarily prepared to understand and appreciate every liberal arts idea offered in college. Adulthood is the ongoing crucible of increasing maturity opening the doors for greater and deeper understanding of the liberal arts. The pains, hard-knocks, tests, and hardships which try the soul and help us grow spiritually, emotionally, and mentally, comprise the theater of human drama helping us see the meaning of general education. Lectures and good teaching during the college years cannot do in two years what life can in a lifetime.

A professor of English once mentioned in a conversation with me that undergraduates often do not have the capability to grasp some literature. He did not mention specific titles, but said students had told him several years after graduation that some books which were difficult to understand during college, become clearer after the students had spent some time in life.

2. Disciplines Overlap

Liberal arts helps us see that disciplines or specialized areas of study overlap. Disciplines are never isolated from each other. The emphasis on specialization grows out of the perceived notion that having a job is so crucial that liberal arts only impedes specialized study and the search for work. The idea that students need only those courses and programs leading to work and money can result in the strictly vocation-orientation of a school. Schools might offer only business, law, computing, and other topics where society thinks job opportunities abound outside academia. Students can be discouraged from majoring in English, philosophy, sociology, and those fields where nonacademic, nonteaching openings seem rare. Specialization without general education can be dangerous in terms of world-view.

Overemphasis on specialization results in compartmentalization. Fragmentation occurs even in colleges and universities with liberal arts programs. The general education programs can become weak and deemphasized. A strong liberal arts may not make a difference. Colleges and universities can encourage students and workers to always study general education in an atmosphere marked by the institution's departments isolated from each other.

The true liberal arts vision means that departments ought respect each other, interrelate, and deny that they are isolated or compartmentalized. General education's purpose must manifest itself continually in departmental world-views as well as in the existence of a liberal arts program. Russell L. Ackoff says that we must never think that nature is compartmentalized in the way that university departments are organized.[4] Nature is not land, water, and air juxtaposed to each other as discreet entities. Nature is a land-water-air whole in movement. A university or college is not physics, chemistry, and other specialties as discreet, airtight departments juxtaposed to each other. Departmentalization involves professors identified with their departments and rarely as interdisciplinary.[5] University and college departments are physics-chemistry-theology-mathematics-philosophy-etc. wholes evolving.

Alfred North Whitehead does not like what he sees in higher education. He warns against biology, language, geometry, algebra, and other courses and disciplines being taught as though no field relates to another field.[6] Unrelated fields are inert ideas. All fields overlap and say something about each other. Henry Winthrop warns that colleges and universities can have stiff liberal arts requirements along with departments seeing themselves as fundamentally unrelated to each other.[7]

Interdisciplinary appreciation among disciplinarians is often called cross-disciplinarity. Alfred North Whitehead, Russell L. Ackoff, and Henry Winthrop would be thrilled to read Jamie Chamberlin's[8] account about cross-disciplinary goals of Patricia Devine. Jamie Chamberlin tells of Patricia Devine's efforts to encourage psychologists to participate in cross-disciplinary research. For example, research into social psychology should show how that field relates to sociology and anthropology. Many mathematicians[9] fear that their discipline is becoming isolated from the real world and other disciplines. At MIT, West Point, and Rochester Institute of Technology, mathematicians are attempting to connect with other departments including biology, physics, and engineering.

George Waltz[10] asks Vannevar Bush about specialization and communication among specialists. Vannevar Bush replies that interdisciplinary communication is critical. The lacking of interdisciplinary communication reduces disciplines to inert ideas. At MIT, engineers must study topics including psychology and economics. No engineer is reducible to a nuts and bolts technician. Every engineer must be a holistic intellectual understanding something of the nonengineering disciplines including sociology and economics.

Earl J. McGrath says liberal arts are foundations of vocationalism and departmentalization.[11] Liberal arts enable us to be interdisciplinarians and not just disciplinary technocrats with tunnel vision. Tunnel vision involves compartmentalization. Tunnel vision ignores that point that vocations change from within, many become obsolete, and that general education enables students to learn fundamental skills preparing them for new challenges that vocationalism and departmentalization cannot.

3. Disciplinarians Are Socially Skilled

Liberal is always telling disciplinarians to be human beings. The holistic approach to disciplines involves telling disciplinarians to respect each others specialization. The holistic liberal arts approach also means that whatever our job, specialists must be human beings and socially skilled.

In his *Out of My Later Years*,[12] Albert Einstein stresses general education. He says schools should emphasize general education and never put it second to specialized study. Albert Einstein points out that specialists should seek a harmonious personality reflecting the evolving wholeness of existence. Human beings are evolving wholes and never specialists, however interdisciplinary, seeing only the intellectual side of human existence.[13] From the perspective of Albert Einstein, life is a rich, multidimensional whole which we cannot restrict to the confines of cognitive disciplinarity. Specialists are more than producers and competent technicians. They are human beings who require liberal arts as well as specialized study. Human beings are fundamentally liberally educated workers or specialists and never just specialists.

Increasing numbers of lifelong learners turn to liberal arts for orientation, values, and ethics underlying specialization. Peter Drucker makes a point about returning students wishing to study liberal arts as well as technical skills. He notes that ongoing learning must be humanizing and liberal as well as vocational.[14] From the perspective of Peter Drucker, lifelong learning is necessary for an increasingly complex industrial society demanding ever more competent professionals who are first of all liberal arts people and human beings.

The term "liberal arts" began as an unfortunate idea. The Latin notion of *artes liberalis* was separate from *artes servilis*. *Artes liberalis* or liberal arts distinguished music and mathematics from the *artes servilis* or servile arts including manual labor. Liberal arts was introduced as an elitist, what I would call classist idea. The wealthy class studied liberal arts in order to remain free from the manual arts of the slaves and manual laborers. Liberal arts were not meant to unify anything. They were intended only to distinguish the workers from the elite who did not work. Today, general education is meant to be more than learning a trade or for a job. Liberal arts gives a holistic, interdisciplinary vision to disciplines. Modern workers need not be slaves or manual laborers. They can be accountants, engineers, musicians, artists, psychologists, and other intellectuals and nonintellectuals. Their common thread is that everyone works and earns a living. Everyone also needs to see all professions as interrelating.

Liberal arts had denoted an *us versus them* mentality. The elite studied liberal arts to remain free from work, free from the *them* or slaves and manual laborers who worked. Our notion of general education is different. People study liberal arts to unify the arts and sciences, to see themselves as human beings and as just workers, to see that all human beings are equal.

Lifelong learning says work and learning are always important. Lifelong learning says education involves learning for a intellectual and nonintellectual careers, and for a holistic perspective to discern the thematic ideas underlying all jobs.

The holistic perspective comprises our notion of liberal arts. General education concerns the foundations of work but does not denounce any career. Stuart Chase[15] says the higher you go on the organizational ladder, the more you need social skills. Any corporation's highest executives must be sensitive to people and understand values.

Ram Charan[16] says CEOs (Chief Executive Officers) fail due to people and character problems, not lack of specialization skills. CEOs who fail do so because of their inability or refusal to see the human forest for the technical trees. The CEOs are fired or quit because of their inability or refusal to work with people and ideas. None of the CEOs who fell from their positions did so because of a lack of encyclopediac knowledge. None of them came down due to lack of specialization. They may be very good in finance, engineering, purchasing, computer science, and other fields. Their downfall is caused in large part due to not working with groups of often competing people, not leading, not showing their presence and intention to guide the organization. The CEOs fail because they do not continually learn about and act on their companies' good and bad news, do not monitor what is happening to the people and events within their control. Commitment, follow through, decisiveness, and sensitivity are as important as knowledge.

Character, values, and morals are fundamental to success, moreso than technical knowledge. Betsey Morris and Patricia Sellers[17] write that character flaws and insensitivity to workers, not the lack of specialized knowledge, results in the firing of Coca Cola CEO, Doug Ivestor. He was fired because of his arrogance, unwillingness to take advice, response late to a crisis in which children got sick drinking Coke, and failure to see the larger picture though he had all the data.[18] The most well-informed CEOs who cannot deal with human beings and be honest to themselves, will fall from the top.

Liberal arts says all members of organizations must be socially skilled. Everyone must know people as well as being specialist. Communicating with colleagues is fundamental to any profession's technical skills. Susan M. Rakley[19] writes that being an M.D. involves appropriate interpersonal relations with everyone including fellow medical personnel.

Physicians and surgeons should know their medicine. They must also understand and practice proper social skills with their co-workers. Bedside manners are needed for working with patients; office manners are required for dealing with all co-workers. Workers from CEOs on down must communicate with each other by considering the other person as what Martin Buber calls a Thou[20] and not an object. Good communication among people emerges from a feeling of mutual respect and is irreducible to what I call inert conversation: demanding, yelling, and otherwise reading people the riot act. I find it interesting that convicted Unabomber, Theodore J. Kaczynski was a brilliant mathematician who could get tenure and a full professorship at Berkeley, but gave it all up because he hated people and could not get along with anyone.

Professionals must communicate in order to get their jobs done. Technical training alone cannot get a job done. Communication excludes reading the riot act when talking. Listening, sympathizing, empathizing, and otherwising taking fellow workers into account are key ingredients for successful professionalism.

Madeleine Jacobs[21] points out that employers look for values as well as technical competence in new applicants. Values are critical from the level of the CEO down to the entry level, and to the stage of the recruit. Workers must be sensitive to their fellow human beings and co-workers whether the workers are CEOs or the newest employee, or applicant. Graduating students should show honesty, integrity, straightforwardness, and loyalty as well as professional skills. Dishonest, disloyal, selfish, and otherwise valueless workers can and will harm their employers and often themselves. The lack of honesty, integrity, straightforwardness, and loyalty could lead to geniuses turning to criminal activity within their professions and industries. Such geniuses could also have a negative impact outside their jobs and within society. Every profession is more than a technical or economic activity.

Studying the liberal arts and sciences on an ongoing basis provides the insights to appreciate and cope with life's manifold manifestations. Life is determination, empathy, and seeing the forest as well as the study of a specialty, and a high intelligence quotient.

Arguing that students must always study general education is not difficult to justify. Workers are rarely working alone. When they work in their own company or as consultants, they continue to interrelate with labor and management in organizations. Such interaction involves more than studying a specialty. Evolving interaction means understanding people, events, and change. Evolving interrelations mean empathy and interpersonal growth. Specialists who refuse to acknowledge the role of values and ethics in their fields are guilty of believing in inert ideas.

4. General Education Is Homological

Wholeness in liberal arts sounds redundent. Liberal arts or general education is supposed to denote the holistic context underlying specialization. General education gives unity to the arts and sciences, to specialization. In principle, general education means wholeness underlying specialization. Such wholeness is empty if general education is reducible to the sum of introductory or survey courses borrowed from the various arts and sciences. General education must be homological.

What constitute general education's structure? My previous two sections indicated that liberal arts helps students and professors communicate interdepartmentally and develop social skills regardless of department. Departmentalization and compartmentalization are wrong. Even in interdepartmental communications on cognitive level, lack of social skills are wrong. My present section says that liberal arts is homological and not the sum of isolated survey or introductory courses borrowed from even the most interrelating departments or disciplines.

Inside liberal arts, the homological approach to liberal arts is lifelong. Students must always study a holistic general education consisting of isomorphies or homologies comprising liberal arts. Lifelong liberal arts would be wrong if it consists of a juxtaposition of isolated courses drawn from separate disciplines. Liberal arts is a dynamic, evolving process of isomorphic, homological wholes as values unfolding as life.

The International Society for Systems Sciences (ISSS) does research into isomorphies or homologies underlying the arts and sciences. This Society can well become part of the foundations of general education. If liberal arts seeks to develop a holistic vision of isomorphies common to the arts and sciences, or to any two or three disciplines, the ISSS provides such insights. The ISSS does not offer ideas about how to juxtapose introductory or survey courses borrowed from special disciplines and unrelated to each other. ISSS offers ideas on themes and structures common to various disciplines.

Students are human beings and need the homological approach to general education. Homologies or isomorphies humanize general education. Evolving, generalist, homological human beings study the liberal arts and sciences. Homologies rehumanize general education by revealing the holistic, evolving nature of knowledge.

Colleges and universities divide knowledge into disciplinary departments. We see chemistry, philosophy, education, mathematics, history, and other departments. Students are admitted into the department (departments if they have a double major) of their choice, representing their career selection. Undergraduates study in the physics department to become physicists, biology to become biologists, psychology department to become psychologists.

The departmental organization influences liberal arts education. General education consists of a course in history, mathematics, psychology, and so on. Students in general education may be given a choice between art and history, between chemistry and biology. The choice is based on the notion that with so many departments, even one course from each would mean too many for the limited time students have for general education.

I said toward the beginning of this chapter that Russell L. Ackoff admonishes us that nature is not compartmentalized the way universities are compartmentalized. I would add that nature is not compartmentalized as are so many general education programs.

Henry Winthrop[22] says general education's traditional format juxtaposing introductory courses from a variety of disciplines cannot provide a unified perspective for the disciplines. The traditional format presents undergraduates with only a chrestomathy of unrelated fields, leaving the undergraduate as a sciolist and not a whole person. General education's wholeness is not comprised of a survey course unrelated to each other, and each taught by specialists in their fields. Students do not receive a holistic perspective of reality by studying introductory courses from psychology, biology, physics, history, mathematics, and so on. In the typical fashion of most general education programs, professors do not indicate to their students how their courses and fields comprise a general liberal arts unity underlying the arts and sciences.

Wholeness involves underlying homologies running throughout all arts and sciences. The thematic, homological, or isomorphic approach provide students with a holistic, value-laden approach cutting across all boundaries between the arts and sciences. The Association for Integrative Studies is involved in developing general education programs along thematic, structured lines. The chapters of my present book constitute some basic isomorphies or homologies underlying all disciplines. Each articlates an aspect of lifelong learning. I spell this out later in this chapter.

Gerald Graff argues for thematic, holistic, evolving approaches to the liberal arts. He opposes fragmentation as when liberal arts comprises a course in psychology, one in physics, another in history, and so on.[23] College, graduate, and lifelong learning students need a holistic perspective integrating the arts and sciences. The holistic view, based on thematic values and process, cannot be achieved when psychology professors teach a liberal arts or general education introductory psychology course never touching on physics, biology, mathematics, history, philosophy, or other disciplines. A holistic view cannot be achieved when chemistry, history, biology, or art professors teach as part of liberal arts their own introductory courses never touching on other disciplines.

Alfred North Whitehead warns against teaching history, language, algebra, and science in such a way that no subject-matter follows from the other.[24] From the perspective of Alfred North Whitehead, we need to see life in all its manifestations.[25] Life in all its manifestations means a course touching on human beings, on all reality, as artistic-scientific. That view indicates that art is scientific and science is artistic. The humanities consist of numeric aspects, and science and technology are oriented around human beings.

I referred earlier in this chapter to Alfred North Whitehead's warning against university and college departments not following from each other. My present one paraphrases him in terms of general education. We need be careful also to see that topics and ideas in the liberal arts follow each other. General education programs should avoid the juxtposition of unrelated introductory courses borrowed from various fields and which never follow from each other. Thematic, isomorphic orientations in general education allow instructors to touch on the arts and sciences in most of their class sessions.

Henry Winthrop warns that nature is not fragmented as are general education programs reducible to the juxtaposition of unrelated introductory courses collected from various disciplines.[26] His words about fragmentation in liberal arts curricula parallel Russell L. Ackoff's warning that nature is not compartmentalized the way university departments are fragmented.[27] Ackoff would concur that nature is not fragmented into a collection of introductory courses in the way many liberal arts programs teach. He would agree with The Association for Integrative Studies, Henry Winthrop, Alfred North Whitehead, myself, and others, that the thematic, homological approach best constitutes the holistic perspective for general education.

Existence or careers comprise various and diverse aspects. We need biologists, psychologists, historians, and other specialists in order to grasp reality's many manifestations. These manifestations find meaning only in a holistic context of values found in liberal arts. To understand a pre-differentiated unity, we differentiate the whole into relatively different parts. At the same time, to understand why and how the parts function, we must always refer to the evolving, ongoing pre-differentiated whole consistently underlying the parts. We do not just cut reality into static parts and juxtapose these inherently unrelated entities into a reducible whole.

Herbert W. Richardson speaks of henology as the study of irreducible unity among disciplines.[28] We cannot be satisfied with knowledge broken up into separate, self-contains disciplines. Herbert W. Richardson argues for a unity which transcends special fields and shows the various specialties as particular manifestations of a fundamental, homological whole. From his perspective, meta-disciplines comprise such a homological view. Meta-mathematics, meta-language, meta-history, meta-ethics, and so on, constitute a critical analysis of particular disciplinary methods and approaches. We attempt to understand why special fields exist and what each attempts to do.

Applied ethics is another movement showing that the isomorphy of morality and values underlies different fields. Business ethics, engineering ethics, legal ethics, medical ethics, bioethics, and so on, indicate that ethics and values are basic or at least part of various arts and sciences.

Kenneth E. Boulding's *The Image* is a good look at what he calls "eiconics"[29] as fundamental to various disciplines. Disciplines consist of eiconic wholes or subjective orientations coloring our perceptions. We do not perceive pristine data and then gather them into objective wholes that exist external to the perceiver. Each discipline is a certain direction and not just isolated questions and answers. Knowledge is the relating of these disciplines. Wholeness in general express human beings and underlies the disciplines by telling us that reality and knowledge mirror the changing social milieu. People do not experience reality and knowledge in terms of mutually exclusive times and spaces. We continue from day to day, from place to place.

Kenneth E. Boulding says the image of wholes we have underly and tie together various disciplines. Kenneth E. Boulding's idea is that our image of events, people, and objects, direct us toward reacting to and often shaping those processes. We behave in the arts and sciences, in any job, in terms of our images, values, and ethics. Liberals and conservatives look at the world and see the same thing: people in need, others who do not need. Political views guide perceptions. Liberals argue that we must help people in need by providing them with material and other necessities. Conservatives suggest that we must help people in need by teaching them to take responsibility for their actions and do the correct things. He likes what Norbert Weiner does in *Cybernetics*.

Cybernetics[30] means organisms are based on the idea of feedback. Organisms continue to exist by adjusting to their environments. We understand the world of organisms by understanding the principle of feedback constituting any evolving organism. The evolution from feedback alone to feedback-feedforward means that organisms can be defined as predictors as well as adjustors.[31]

Alfred North Whitehead says we gain the greatest knowledge through the simplest apparatus.[32] The greatest understanding does not occur by fragmented views juxtaposing introductory chemistry, biology, mathematics, history, and so on lacking an inherently continuous, coherent context. Deeper understanding occurs through the simpler, homological apparatus underlying different disciplines. The simplest apparatus consists of understanding structural similarities underlying the arts and sciences.

Alfred North Whitehead's idea of philosophy as the critique of abstractions can provide part of that picture.[33] Philosophy as critique of abstractions provides that simplest apparatus. As critique, philosophy is the underlying context in which abstractions make sense. In the present context, abstractions are the various arts and sciences. Philosophy is homological, underlying all the arts and sciences, by showing that structural similarities comprise knowledge. The major similarity is that knowledge and reality are evolving and in process. No disciplinary borders, no human being, remain as unaffected, static entities. Alfred North Whitehead breaks ground for philosophy as the liberating art and science. Our inherent vision says that we need to abstract or analyze reality in terms of its parts, but must then always reintegrate parts in terms of the isomorphic whole. The present chapter means isomorphic unity amid legitimate disciplines.

Through philosophy as critic of disciplinary abstraction, we understand humanistic context for science. We see and appreciate the evolving unity of biology, chemistry, language, literature, physics, mathemtics, history, religion, psychology, education, and other disciplines. Divided into humanities and sciences, the humanities provide the human foundations of reduction. The basic humanities, philosophy, enables each discipline to speak of its contribution to the whole, and its part in manifesting the whole. Physics shows physical laws, and how these fit into a knowledge of human nature and reality. Biology reveals biological laws, and how they fit into a total knowledge of human nature and reality. No discipline is inherently unrelated to others. Each discipline manifests a particular way in which an interdisciplinary homology or isomorphy evolves as intellectual unity.

Herbert Richardson speaks of henology and meta-disciplinary instead of reductively disciplinary thinking. Scholars do not first institute a discipline and then attempt to relate it to other fields. All disciplines emerge from the human experience.

My present book is a homological approach to liberal arts. Liberal arts is responsible for outlining the homologies underlying the arts and sciences. General education becomes the focal point or vehicle for pointing out the directions of lifelong learning. I do not find that responsibility surprising, since general education is wholeness and values.

This chapter is a homology: all arts and sciences, all jobs, manifest the homology or isomorphy of lifelong liberal arts. To the extent that liberal arts presents an overview of the homologies underlying art and science, the present chapter is meta-homological. The present chapter says that this book's chapters are interrelated and not inert ideas superficially juxtaposed to each other. General education is the isomorphy that says we need to study at least eight isomorphies including lifelong liberal education. The eight homologies are: (1) lifelong learning, (2) lifelong community in distance learning, (3) lifelong classroom for most teaching, (4) lifelong simplication of the information explosion, (5) lifelong liberal arts, (6) lifelong thinking about specialized motions, (7) lifelong theory for data.

I propose liberal arts as lifelong study of homologies underlying jobs. Each chapter in my present book shows an homology. Whatever your career, you need to learn always, think about specialization and specialized study, think about activity within a given discipline, understand unity, the data-theory continuum, the information explosion, distance learning and so on.

Jobs are not just technical knowledge. Each job, each art and science, manifests general homologies. Some ideas are found in every job. Each job is the particular manifestation of general ideas. In any occupation, learning, the liberal arts, intradisciplinary thinking, theory, simplifying the information explosion, community within distance learning, community and cyberspace, and community within the traditional classroom, are all lifelong.

We learn to always learn. Whatever our jobs, learning never stops. Work and learning alternate throughout life.

We learn to always rehumanize interactive distance learning.

We learn to always return to the classroom and not replace it with the Internet or even interactive distance learning.

We learn to constantly simplify the information explosion. Knowledge is not quantity of data, theory, or multiplicity of theory. Scholars ought not juxtapose data to data, theory to theory in getting to knowledge. Simplicity is still a-b-c-d in disciplines and general education. Students must study an increasingly complex general education orienting a similarly complex picture of specialization and subspecialization. Since learning is lifelong, this complexity can be slowly understood over time.

We learn to always learn liberal arts underlying specialized study. Whatever our jobs, the liberal arts are continually relevant. Departments are not a *and* b *and* c. They are a-b-c.

We learn to always learn homological liberal art. Not just liberal arts in name. That can mean juxtoposed, isolated courses. We propose themes and reject isolated courses and subject-matter not following from each other, and the other extreme of simplistic liberal arts unrelated to the word.

We learn to continually learn to think about our motions. Every job requires thinking about what we are doing.

We learn to always learn theory underlying data. In any occupation, theoretical orientation gives meaning to data and research. We never start with data in order to find theory; totally objective data does not exist.

Finally, we learn to always be vigilant against inert ideas clogging our educational system. We need to be as careful about inert ideas starting in the educational system and spreading throughout society, as we are about contagious disease anywhere.

Interdisciplinarity is never automatically holistic. Juxtaposing different disciplinary courses or ideas lacking homological unity becomes inert ideas. Unity amid discplines is fundamentally irreducible to the superficial sum total of parts taken from various cognitive fields. Holistic interdisciplinarity involves a basic perspective involving general ideas of which specific disciplines are limited expressions. Disciplines are the variety of ways in which wholeness unfolds.

5. Liberal Arts as Foresight

Liberal arts tells students to be evolving, holistic human beings and workers. As evolving, holistic human beings who work, students have the responsibility with instructors to consider the ethics of work.

General education provides students with the insights which enable them to develop new skills before employers establish new jobs. Liberal arts also provide students with the opportunity to drop outdated abilities before employers jettison the jobs having required those abilities.

Alfred North Whitehead uses an intriguing metaphor to define philosophy. Philosophy builds cathedrals before bricklayers have moved the first brick into place, and tears down these edifices before the laborers have removed the first stones from those buildings.[34]

Philosophy and liberal arts are related in their purpose of foreseeing and predicting the vocational future. Building cathedrals before bricklayers have moved the first brick into position, or tearing them down before wreckers have removed the first brick from its place, constitutes philosophical direction for the bricklayers. Liberal arts helps us understand why we study a certain field, how that field changes, disappears, and is replaced by other fields. General education does all this before students experience problems in the workplace.

Learning to be an expert bricklayer does not guarantee that the construction industry will always remain the same. The industry can decrease in size and many bricklayers will find themselves unemployed. Learning to be an expert in anything means lifelong preparation for changes in any vocation.

Alfred North Whitehead's cathedral metaphor raises two related questions. Is philosophy of education the same as philosophy? Is philosophy of education fundamental to understanding philosophy? Alfred North Whitehead is not explicit about the relation, but John Dewey,[35] Robert Maynard Hutchins,[36] and I would concur that philosophy of education is essential to understanding philosophy. Philosophy helps us anticipate what will occur by enabling us to look at situations in their holistic contexts. Past, present, and future are integrated. In looking at situations holistically and learning, we are doing a philosophy of education. Whether we are first or essentially doing philosophy or philosophy of education may be difficult to asses, since both are strongly interrelated. My point is that philosophy and philosophy of education are not two distinct ideas. We do not have philosophy as a field of study, and then see philosophy of education simply among many branches within that field.

Students in college may major in philosophy, and most students must take a required philosophy course. Traditionally, philosophy majors and other students need not study philosophy of education as undergraduates. Philosophy of education is reserved for education students. A deeper insight into philosophy of education and philosophy as holistic, evolving consideration of values and the world can justify philosophy of education as crucial to studying philosophy and the arts and sciences.

Separating philosophy from the philosophy of education implies that philosophy of education is only one branch of philosophy. Alfred North Whitehead's metaphor may be interpreted as suggesting that educational philosophy is philosophy, that philosophy is educational philosophy. Education and philosophy enable people to learn and grow as human beings, as human becomings. Learning is the total, fundamental, philosophical experience of seeing existence as values evolving as wholes.

Bringing philosophy and education so close to each other means that philosophy, philosophy of education, and education are essentially liberal arts. Philosophical and educational foundations of specialized study provide students with the holistic vision of the lifelong updating of skills before those abilities are required in the workforce.

Cybernetics, mentioned above, is another field very close to educational philosophy and philosophy. Philosophy and philosophy of education help students foresee and have some control over their careers. Cybernetics speaks of people being controlled by and yet having considerable control over events.

The idea of feedback has been central to the traditional idea of education before lifelong learning. Workers react, often negatively and to job changes. They have no control over what occurs in the workforce. Lifelong learning gives them power and insight in the workforce. Ongoing education allows workers to foresee and control their employment destiny. Lifelong learning practices the next step in the evolution of cybernetics.

We have the ability to build cathedrals before we move the first brick into place, and tear down cathedrals before we remove the first brick from the edifice. In feedforward, lifelong learning as liberal arts helps us see which professions will appear, disappear, and change from within. Feedback means people have no control in manipulating events; events shape people. Feedforward means people have increasing control in directing events; people can shape events more and more.

At MIT, students learn to think about doing.[37] MIT is saying that we must integrate the laboratory and classroom within a discipline. I shall explicate this in my next chapter. My present chapter interprets thinking about doing in terms of liberal arts as thinking and the study of specialization as doing. Fragmenting thinking from doing reduces thought and action to inert ideas.

In the broadest sense, general educations tells us to think about our and any specialty. Studying our future profession, becoming learned in biology, chemistry, mathematics, history, theology, English, and so on, is not enough. The holistic perspective means thinking about or understanding how and why disciplines emerge, change, disappear, and contribute to the total view of human nature. As we think about doing in terms of studying specialized fields, our approach helps us see them as cognitive areas being studied by human beings who are more than cognitive or technical. Human beings are also involved in human relations.

If cybernetics, philosophy, and philosophy of education help students see what jobs and specialized study will disappear and which changes will occur, we must ask deeper questions. Which professions ought to disappear and which appear? What skills within remaining professions ought to be jettisoned and what abilities ought appear? Ethics becomes the foundations and nature of philosophy, education, liberal arts, and lifelong learning.

6. What Jobs Ought To Exist?

General education, philosophy, and philosophy of education help workers foresee and deal with the future. Alfred North Whitehead's metaphor of the cathedral and philosophy, and the idea of feedforward cybernetics involve general education's ability to anticipate vocational uncertainties. Beyond the ability to foresee change, dealing with job loss, creation, and evolution is an ethical issue. We need to think about values: what types of jobs ought exist?

Work is social. Sociologist of work, Fred Davis[38] would say that liberal arts provide the non-instrumental values orienting the instrumental knowledge gained in specialized study.

The non-instrumental is the non-productive or the pre-productive value underlying profuctivity. Non-instrumentality can mean our values and ethics concerning which jobs we jettison. Before we develop a new job, get rid of or change an existing field of work, we must ask if the new profession is ethical. We need to ask whether getting rid of the old occupation is morally justified.

Work is more than the crass production of goods and services. Human values are fundamental in creating, jwettisoning, or changing jobs.

New jobs are not ethical if they are only ways of producing goods and services apart from the social dimension. Existing jobs ought not be removed if they provide humane work opportunities for people. New jobs are of no value if they do away with or degrade human dignity.

Jerome B. Wiesner[40] says that human beings have undergone an ethical and technical evolution. We have evolved from the inability to control life, and toward the ability to intervene to improve existence. We are at the stage where we can do good or ill to ourselves.

Scientific tools unheard of decades ago allow uas to make ethical and unethical decisions. These decisions include job creatioin, elimination, and change.

Job creation, loss, and evolution require the holistic perspective. A *Chicago Sun-Times*[41] article and a *Chicago Tribune*[42] article talk of nuances, complexities, and values of creating and losing jobs. The president of the United States takes credit for creating 20 million new jobs.[43] Creation of jobs lowers unemployment. The president likes to speak in simplistic sound-bites. Some of these oversimplificatiions involve the point that our leaders are creating jobs.

Many people want to hear that we now have more jobs than before. These persons see life and work in black and white, nuance-, and value-free terms. They believe that more jobs mean a better life, and fewer jobs mean a less acceptable quality of life.

The bigger picture of jobs involves ethics or values. Bureaucratic jobs should be reduced. These reduce workers and clients to numbers. Governmental and corporate bureaucracies serve no humane purpose. Jobs paying less than living wages need be eliminated or their pay increased. Dehumanizing fields of work need to be eliminated to rehumanized.

Ethics thinkers including myself are concerned with exploring job changes within the context of wholeness and values. Scholars must educate the public and each other that job creation, loss, and evolution ought be within the context of human dignity.

Oversimplified presidential and other political proclamations extolling new jobs represent inert ideas. Books such as my present work correct those inert ideas with the holistic perspective of work.

Lifelong learning says that things are always changing. Tomorrow can bring work the likes of which we cannot imagine. I argue that we must develop a sense of community and values underlying the creation, loss, and evolution of jobs. We cannot be satisfied with the purely statistical "is" telling the world that more and more jobs are emerging. Scholars must redirect society toward the ethical or "ought" whereby we can focus on what jobs need to exist, which to discard, and how humanizing jobs can and must evolve.

When we create new jobs, our values will guide us so that we do not establish careers heretofore illegal, immoral, and otherwise dehumanizing. The sociology of work tells us that work or productivity is a human activity irreducible to mechanical production. Paul Davis mentioned above, is saying that work is more than "doing." Establishing job fields for the sake of low unemployment means that we can have dehumanizing, socially unacceptable jobs.

If we say that unemployment is down, or, say, zero, lots of people would be happy. The president of the United States would be very happy. That happiness implies that job in the generic sense is good. My point is that unemployment can be zero and lots of people can be working in unethical occupations, unsafe workplaces, making very low wages, and so on.

We must ask if workers are working in socially desirable jobs, in safe workplaces, and earning a decent living. Work is socially constrained and expresses values of human becomings instead of crass production. If work is dehumanized productivity, lots of jobs are possible and society suffers in the long-term because people are doing dehumanizing work.

Slavery means people produce without life, liberty, and the pursuit of happiness. We outlaw slavery because slaves produce without being acknowledged as human beings. They work for persons who are called masters or slave owners and never reap the benefits of their labor. People should not own other people. Being a boss or even Chief Executive Officer (CEO) is one thing. Owning a worker is another thing.

The totally automated workplace is another option. We have a choice of creating a factories where machines do all the work. History has shown that we once lived in the rainforest. The rainforest was a reality. People lived like that in ancient times. Total automation as the opposite may be impossible. Complete automation is unethical even if possible. Weisner says we can now choose. Work is not just a mechanical activity producing goods and services. Production is a human activity involving human becomings and irreducible to mechanical motions.

Gambling and other previously and currently illegal activity are legislated as jobs or at least debated. I find it informative that the government makes counterfeiting a crime. We say that inflation is bad because of its economic implictions. Bad money and large quantities of legal currency are wrong because of their harmful effects on the nation. Similarly, we can argue that legalizing a previously illegal career for the sake of jobs and revenue is also ultimately harmful to society. The government is always considering values and community when stating that people may not print their own money and that prices and wages ought not spiral upward. Our government may be secular and consider religious input unnecessary for moral decisions by our leaders. The government's insistence on values concerning counterfeiting and inflation suggests that a secular government continues to acknowledge the need for values.

Internet and e-commerce economics is fast gaining a foothold in society. The Internet could eliminate or diminish bookstores and other kinds of outlets. Traditional shopping involves our interpersonal, physical presence in the social context of work. Shopping in cyberspace must be considered and debated before society decides to eliminate the idea of traditional stores.

Shopping in cyberspace and jettisoning the traditional brick and mortar store is an example of dumping an existing job due to creating a new field: computers. Creating a new field, changing or destroying existing jobs concern values.

We are able to bring or learn to adjust to changes in existing jobs. Our task is to ask if such changes are ethical? Libraries replace card catalogues with computers. Toll roads replace toll booths with IPass cards. These cards do not eliminate traffic conjestion or the need to consider trains and other forms of mass transit. The cards do not develop better ecological perspectives. We are not asking if more roads are necessary, but only can we drive through quicker?

The ethical approach to work tells us to look at a holistic vision underlying the structure of occupations. Let me consider the following.

Hiring must be holistic. One extreme is dehumanized application and hiring. We hire only the qualified. The qualified may be a competent technician and a serious flawed human being such as Theodore J. Kaczynski. Applicants only send in applications, endure interviews, and are hired or rejected on the basis of the purely cognitive and technical. Hiring must allow scholars and others to personally recommend and "feed to" their colleagues those applicants who seem the best.

The other extreme involves bias. The good old boy network can be biased and unfair. Somewhere between the old boy network and merely applying and interviewing, stands the personal approach. Colleagues can suggest several names to each other for employment. We do not just "hire" the "applicant," or hire on the basis of bias. Society must help guide the qualified toward desirable spots.

Hiring must be an ongoing social process of developing people toward jobs. Once people are hired job security must be reasonable. People cannot be totally insecure about being fired. Knowing the organization can fire a worker anytime can be demoralizing. Workers may also not be completely secure. Knowing that an organization cannot fire or discipline them is dangerous to all concerned. Gaining security should be a process. The longer the worker has been working, the more their job security grows. Security must be an lifelong process of developing workers within jobs. If people are misbehaving at work, they should be corrected. If their mistakes and misbehavior are due to their being in the wrong job, being in the right job but having low salaries and other bad working conditions, management should address those issues and not just fire workers.

Management must be humane. Management should not stifle workers or allow anarchy. Administration is a lifelong process of dialogue between worker and boss. Management ought to work with labor and ask for worker input. Executives hurt themselves when they refuse employee input. They hurt themselves if they only go along with anything that employees may demand. The best managers choose an ongoing position between decisiveness that ignores employees and permissiveness that destroys managerial control.

Humane management means reasonable hours. Workers do not just put in so many hours a day, and they do not just call in absent as they feel. Like punishment or education, work is not a matter of putting in time. Incarceration without or in place of rehabilitation proves nothing and can breed recidivism. Refusal to punish when punishment is due can result in higher crime rates. Education should not mean just putting time in school, or eliminating education. Learning is the lifelong process of teacher and student relations. Work is similar. We work reasonable hours for satisfying productivity. Putting in hours does not satisfy long-term productivity or national health. A nation without work becomes poverty stricken and decadent.

Working overtime only because so much work exists and demands our time, requires rethinking. Work is always here. Work always needs to be done. The requirement to work cannot mean that people need to put in more and more hours without ever leaving the workplace, or need to bring the work home and never have a life outside work. Jobs do not denote constant production. What about pay?

Pay should be tied to satisfaction. Pay is irreducible to money. Money is necessary. A salary without satisfaction becomes the sole, external compensation for work. Somewhere between mere money and a subsistence wage, pay must be reasonable, always within the context of a person's satisfaction with the job.

The world's highest employment rate does no good if jobs pay less than a living wage, or if pay is the only incentive for work. The amount of money workers receive is a constantly challenging idea where evolving conditions demand the awareness of human rights and labor responsibilities.

Our values and the holistic vision tell us that the externals of work as a social activity, legality, hiring, pay, hours, management, and security, manifest the human context. We do not just study to work, work at an illegal job, be hired, payed, put in hours, earn job security. To only be hired, and so on, means that we are satisfying impersonal, dehumanizing processes and not growing as human beings. Work that lacks ethics, values, and a humane vision becomes inert ideas.

7. Changing Jobs

Wilbur J. Cohen[41] says that people going to college and graduate schools should not expect to remain in the same job their entire lives. We need to put his statement into context.

We cannot universalize his words. Jobs change, disappear, and new ones emerge. Some jobs will remain, including medicine, police, and aviation. Some professionals should remain and evolve in their areas of work. Doctors, pilots, and police do not have to plan for having two or three different careers until retirement. The expertize with which they can be increasingly productive will require decades of evolving experience. People who can change careers might include bank workers becoming clergy, clergy becoming computer workers, computer workers going over to banking, bus drivers becoming electrical workers or carpenters, and the like.

Some persons can successfully change fields before retirement. Their successes do not depend on decades of experience. Bank officials become clergy, construction workers enter law enforcement.

Learning and thinking throughout life do not mean having to change careers. Workers remaining in their fields can and do change or evolve to become better at what they do. Their rethinking and returning to school enables them to relearn what to do better before those innovations emerge in their work. When educators tell us that workers in modern society will rarely remain in the same field until retirement, their words should be read carefully.

Traditional workers remained in the same field their entire lives. The problem is that knowledge and work never evolved. Lifelong learning has meant that every worker ought to return to school to relearn and rethink changes in jobs that are not disappearing. As a reaction to the traditional image of working in the same field until retirement, lifelong learning tells workers to be more adjustible. Adjustibility means all workers change, some leaving their careers, other evolving within their professions.

Physicians, pilots, some teachers, and police are professionals who should remain in their fields for prolonged experience and expertize. Good physicians and police get to grow with experience and time. Physicians become more communal with their patients, police get to know criminality and how criminals behave. We cannot make a crass statement that every worker will or must change careers during their life.

Some people can successfully remain in their fields until retirement. They should do so for increasing competence. Police investigators gain more experience as time goes on. Pilots become better acquainted and competent as they fly more. Medical specialists gain more experience and insight with time. I do not see an experienced cardiologist becoming an ophthalmologist, pilot, law enforcement officer, or diamond specialist.

8. Preventing Starvation

Alfred North Whitehead's idea of philosophy building cathedrals before bricklayers have moved the first brick into position, or tearing down cathedrals before the laborers have removed the first brick from the building, has substantial meaning.

We like to think of the bricklayer as earning a living and not starving. Similarly, we do not think of the architects, executives, and other non-bricklayers as starving. Liberal arts do not make students starve. General education helps students foresee jobs becoming obsolete before those jobs are lost. General education also helps students learn newer skills before they may be in demand. Additionally, by teaching values and morals, liberal arts helps students learn about themselves, about integrity, the work ethic, honesty, and related non-instrumentalities enabling them to be better workers.

Pre-instrumentality in terms of learning does not mean that workers starve as they pause to return to school. Pre-instrumental study as liberal arts would not denote that students will starve if they study general education in school, along with specialized study.

Robert Maynard Hutchins is a major advocate for liberal arts and science. He says general education should be taught in college and throughout lifelong learning. Students do not pull their punches in attacking Robert Maynard Hutchins for defending liberal arts. Students criticize him for his stand by saying that they would all starve to death if they adopted his ideas.[45] Their view is that work is so central to life that education must train students for a job. If learning does not mean only studying a specialty, then the educational system fails and society falls apart because people are not prepared for working. Robert Maynard Hutchins reacts to this vocational view.

He argues that we will starve to death if we do not learn the liberal arts and sciences. In a changing world where technology is making so many jobs disappear rightly or wrongly, general education students are able to think about what they are studying as specialists. Students who remain in one field can learn enough to earn a living in that area. What happens if their jobs are lost or radically evolving? Do they possess skills to relearn in current or other areas? They can relearn if they have been taught to relearn constantly.

If students ignore liberal arts in order to specialize for the sake of earning a living, how critical is money in their lives? If pay is the determining factor, are students going to specialize in fields that pay the most money. Carpenters make more than some professors. Will students become carpenters because of the money? Some criminals make more money than good citizens. The fact that crime pays big dividends in many cases is no reason for people to turn to crime.

Taking pay to the logical conclusion, we find an ethical issue. Criminals make more money sometimes than innocent people. Consider the citizen who we do not classify as a criminal. If money is the only issue, will specialists do what they can to rip off the customer? The law calls this price-gauging. Counterfeiting can mean literally making a lot of money without fear of the U.S. Secret Service coming after you. The U.S. Secret Service goes after counterfeiters but not people who charge customers more than they should. Businesspeople who rip-off their customers through price-gauging are not starving to death. They are making a good living through a lot of money. Their living wage is high, but their ethics and morals disappear quickly and society suffers.

Consider demographics and geography. Workers in one area of the country may make earn more than those in other parts of the country. Will specialists travel to the areas where pay is greatest? If they do, they can find that expenses are also greater in those areas. Consider the consequences of moving with the money or following the dollar.

People in New York City can move to Albany, New York because pay is higher in Albany. Residents in New York State can move to Texas for higher salaries. The higher earnings in the new locations are never guaranteed. Economics change. The world is a volatile place. What do workers do when they find earnings drop in the new location? They may seek other locations with high salaries. The attitude to follow the dollar would lead to ridiculous and tragic consequences as workers become nomads for the sake of higher paychecks.

If money is the prime factor, students may choose careers not to their liking or abilities. They will enter because of the pay, and if lucky, not get fired. Students who argue against liberal arts insist that work is so important that they must study only those courses directly leading to a job.

Even if jobs did not become obsolete, workers are basically thinking human beings and must study ideas more basic than what to do at work. If workers have days off during the job-cycle, and return from the work-cycle to the school-cycle, existence is irreducible to work and work irreducible to constant production. We can go one step ahead and argue that knowledge of work, specialized study, is never all that should be studied. Knowledge is irreducible to a specialty.

Six

REHUMANIZING
DISCIPLINARY MOTIONS

My previous chapter justifies the liberal arts. General education is the lifelong foundations of lifelong specialization. Students return to school to relearn specialization. They must return also to relearn values through general education as the ongoing, perennial context for specialized study.

Skills and practicality are part of ongoing learning within specialized study. Even if students always learn to do within a specialized area, they need to also continually think about what they do. Doing without thinking comprises inert ideas. Learning more skills or procedures of a discipline is insufficient. Thinking about skills is lifelong. Lifelong thinking about a discipline's procedures means that students are irreducible to those specialized skills, just as people are irreducible to being specialists. Thinking about doing rehumanizes a specialized field's techniques. Values within a discipline give context and meaning for that discipline's activity. Evolving, generalist human beings who think about doing in specialized study are the people who study specialization's techniques.

1. Disciplinary Cathedrals

Liberal arts tells students to be evolving, holistic human beings and workers. General education speaks also about preventing stagnation in the workforce.

General education provides students with the insights which enable them to develop new skills before employers establish new jobs. Liberal arts also provide students with the opportunity to drop outdated abilities before employers jettison the jobs having required those abilities.

My previous chapter notes Alfred North Whitehead's definition of philosophy by talking of building and tearing down cathedrals. Philosophy builds cathedrals before bricklayers have moved the first brick into place, and tears down these edifices before the laborers have removed the first stones from those buildings.[1]

Learning to be an expert bricklayer does not guarantee that the construction industry will always remain the same. The industry can decrease in size and many bricklayers will find themselves unemployed. Learning to be an expert in anything means lifelong preparation for changes in any vocation.

MIT Students learn to think about job's procedures.[2] MIT says students must think about motions or techniques in any job. Specialists must integrate the laboratory (doing) and classroom (values, thinking) giving context to the laboratory within a discipline. Liberal arts enables students to think about and anticipate the nature, aim, and status of specializations. Within specializations, thinking and values help them to anticipate the nature, aim, and status of motions and practices.

My present chapter says that inside specialized studies, thinking about doing as motions and techniques is lifelong. Thinking about specialized techniques, skills, and procedures never stops. Specialized study requires constant thinking about a discipline's technical side. Thinking about skills, professionalism, and competence within a specialized field is a dynamic, evolving process continuing throughout life.

2. Disciplinary Thinking Never Ends

Specialization can denote doing as working in a career. Liberal arts denotes thinking about how and why careers exist, evolve, and disappear. We would be wrong to assume that specialists only do, and leave thinking to the liberal arts'. Specialization involves technique and activity. These disciplinary, specialized motions, procedures, and ideas require intradisciplinary thinking and values for orientation and improvement. Liberal arts enables students to think about doing as specialization. Inside specialization, disciplinary thinking helps the specializing student to think about doing of motions, techniques, and specialized ideas.

If liberal arts is lifelong interdisciplinary thinking about disciplines, any discipline is comprised of lifelong intradisciplinary thinking about that specialty's motions. Specialists must always think about what and why they do within their specialities. Refusal to think about disciplinary motion reduces that activity to .

3. Motions

Alfred North Whitehead's metaphor of the cathedral applies within disciplines as well as to liberal arts. In terms of liberal arts, we interpret his statement to mean that philosophy builds, changes, and tears down disciplines before employers make the first modifications in jobs. As we speak of disciplines or specialties, the metaphor takes a parallel meaning.

Philosophy, lifelong learning, the philosophy of education, or cybernetics within a given discipline put that specialty's techniques and motions into perspective. We are able to foresee the end of irrelevant motions, the start of new techniques, and changes in traditional activity constituting a discipline. Proactivity in liberal arts has its counterpart in proactivity within a discipline.

Proactivity in liberal arts' involves seeing job creations, disappearance, and evolution before employers bring forth, take away, or innovate within careers.

Proactivity within a given discipline means a discipline or profession enables us to see motions created, disappear, and evolve before employers bring forth, take away, or innovate within that job. Every worker must be a vocational, disciplinary, or specialized thinker as well as doer.

Specialized study is more than performing physical tasks. Thinking about what we do at the workplace is the context for those tasks. We do not just study and practice motions and activity. We think about motions.

Values and ethical constraints guide techniques and motions in the workplace. Fred Davis[3] says that even in a secular society religious orientation may not flourish or influence workers, moral and ethical values continue to exist. Workers are human beings even in the most secular state, and need to express community in and out of workplaces. Values in a secularized civilization may not come down from the Church or religious institutions. Desacralized society looks to social and political philosophies of equity and human decency for treating workers as human beings.

Motions or techniques involved in production comprise the tangible, quantifiable instruments with which to produce goods and services. Fred Davis says that values in the workplace comprise the non-instrumental constraints guiding and motivating such techniques.[4] Instrumentality is always necessary for actual production. Non-instrumental values are equally necessary always for the human context and direction of such production.

An article about the military says soldiers push buttons at work, and learn the reasons for pushing buttons in school.[5] They are continually attending school and relearning why they push buttons. Schools in the military enable personnel to reflect on war, strategy, weapons, history, and various subjects related to confronting battle.

Simulations give military personnel the opportunity to live as realistic a battle situation as possible. When students in the military take part in exercises, they push buttons and do all the other things which would occur in battle. The only thing they do not do is kill another human being or damage property which should not be destroyed. Short of inflicting harm on fellow soldiers and destroying government or private property, soldiers in training and retraining bomb, shoot, and pretend to kill the enemy if our own soldiers are acting as the enemy. In maneuvers, soldiers learn and relearn the actions to do in battle. They also learn to think about those actions.

Let me consider one aspect of the military. Navy SEALs do not just learn to penetrate enemy territory to kill, kidnap, bomb, or collect intelligence. How they enter, perform, survive, evade the enemy, and exit, are keys to their success. In his *SEAL*, Michael J. Walsh, a retired SEAL, explains that thinking is fundamental to every SEAL's training, retraining, and deployment.[6] Every SEAL, he points out, is a thinker.[7] No SEAL only does. Doing is the method of getting things done, of accomplishing missions. Doing cannot accomplish anything if SEALs "do" without thinking about the efficacy and often the ethics of their actions. Values are fundamental to doing, even within the SEALs. Navy SEALs know that thinking underlies combat as well as civilian behavior.

The military expert credited with founding the SEALs was punished for being mission-oriented.[8] Roy Boehm demands that his men do the job regardless of its consequences to them. In giving order and commanding a raid or other mission, he was not concerned with how many men he could lose or whether the mission could be accomplished with minimal casualties. Roy Boehm's only concern was that the mission be carried, and whoever died died. Being aggressive and attempting to lead in combat is desirable. Being so aggressive that the mission orients the warriors instead of values orienting the mission, reduces the mission to suicide and soldiers to dispensible objects. An educational institution attempts to instill values and thought over physical motion.

At MIT, students learn the reasons behind fixing televison sets.[9] Understanding this helps them develop better communications equipment. The ability to use pliers is important. We need to fix broken electronic equipment. More crucially, we need to think about the nature and philosophy of equipment, electronics, physics, and the mathematics which go along with these instruments and ideas. Thinking about the equipment provides the foundations for improving electronics and devices. Sociologist of work, Fred Davis, would call thinking about motions and the prevention of what I term inert motions, as non-instrumental values.

Students learn nothing at MIT and anywhere else if they read and practice with pliers when television technology advances and newer ideas in communications emerge. The nature of the television set, if integrated with the computer, telephone, fax, and email, changes the instrument. Expertize with pliers does not help those who repair television sets to keep their jobs. Thinking about communications and advances in technology will help people keep jobs and survive.

Students at MIT and other colleges and universities study the sciences. Sciences have classrooms and laboratories. Classrooms teach students to think about what they do in laboratories. The theoretical approach in classrooms and practical activity in laboratories mean an integration of the instrumental and non-instrumental. Learning what and how to do in the laboratory is important, but not enough. The lecture or classroom informs students about why they do as they do in the laboratory.

Let us consider cybernetics again. If students learn only in a laboratory and never in class, they are learning about how something works but never why it works and could change. Classroom study of why techniques change, appear, and disappear is fundamental to perfecting the technology in the laboratory. If we only practice a technique in the laboratory, we would have to adjust to the feedback when the technique changes or disappears. Restricting ourselves to the laboratory's practical, immediate perspective forces us to lose sight of the technique's social, scientific, cultural, economic, political, and related non-instrumental dimensions. Instrumental activity always reflects values and ethics. We need to study feedforward.

Thinking about doing within a discipline involves feed forward. The classroom teaches students why they are doing as they do in the laboratory. They can then anticipate, change, and shape the future before it occurs. Ripley Hotch tells the story of Jack Blaeser as CEO of a corporation.[10] Jack Blaeser did not want or expect to become CEO of Concord Communications. When the corporations was going under, he was asked to become the CEO. Reluctantly, he agreed. Among his basic objectives is to have employees ask about what they are doing each day in terms of technique.

Several months after he became CEO, company profits rose and employee morale improved. Jack Blaeser told employees to consider each activity, each technique that they perform. They must than ask whether this technque is correct and why it should occur. If they feel that a technique is not good, they jettison it and not just continue doing without purpose.

Employees at Concord are thinking about what they are doing and not just doing without thinking. Doing without thinking brings in paycheck for a while. After a while, doing things incorrectly or meaninglessly hurts the company and its employees.

A corporation's success or failure can impinge in large part on its willingness to impart values and direction to all people, from CEO on down to the clerical level. Russel V. Gerbman[11] says corporations need to have a lifelong re-orienting educational or learning process for its employees at every level. Such ongoing relearning process gives the workers a sense of company values, direction, meaning, and motivation. Why workers do as they are asked to do is more crucial than telling them what and how they are to perform.

Secret Service Agents constantly return to school to rethink how and why they guard the president of the United States.[12] Guarding the president presents serious challenges to the agents. Among other things, they need to relearn and reinforce the idea of taking a bullet for the president. Human beings do not want to get hurt or die. They are not normally suicidal. Secret Service Agents learn, and relearn, that they must do many difficult things to protect the nation by protecting the president. The government wishes to keep agents from harm's way, and not make agents' lives and work any more dangerous than need be. The nature of the job requires that agents relearn their duties sufficiently well that life need not be taken. Those who threaten the president should be found and apprehended, preventing shootings and other harmful event.

Judges are encouraged to participate in lifelong learning.[13] Law school is not enough to prepare judges for the courtroom. Laws change everyday. Debates, research, Supreme Court and other decisions impact judges' work. Implications about the presence of television cameras in the courtroom influence legal proceedings. Increasing research into DNA raises questions about its applicability in court. Bad judges harm people. Bad agent harms president and nation. Bad soldiers harm nation and self. study specialization not just to do, but to do in human interest. To make world better place for human beings. Juries are a related issue.

Many people constantly attempt to avoid jury duty.[14] Judges and legal scholars continually assess the problems and promises of jury duty. If people are called to jury duty and find the experience a major disruption in their lives, the legal system would need to alter methods of jury selection, seclusion, and the time required for cases to continue until the jury is asked to decide. Jury avoidance is tricky. If a few people dislike something, their attempt to avoid it may be seen as simply personal. They are told that they must do it. If large numbers of people try to avoid somethig, perhaps something must be done to humanize the activity.

Leo Ciaramiaro points out that Duquesne University Law School Dean Emeritus, John Sciullo,[15] argues for legal education as an ongoing learning process and not vocational training for lawyers. John Sciullo argues against narrow legalistic training on criminal and legal procedures. Lawyers must know how to analyze, think, and make ethical judgements. The legal mind should understand the nation's history, culture, and civilization. Changes are being made in medicine as well as law.

We are moving away from reactive to predictive medicine. David Pilling[16] tells of changes in medical diagnosis and treatment. Thanks to developing knowledge of genetics and bodily processes, the future of medicine means we can tap nature bodily processes for regenerating destroyed and degenerating tissues and organs. Transplants may be a relic of the past. The ethics of new medical and biological procedures compel us to think about changes and direct them toward humane aims. We do not succeed as a nation or world by developing the best predictions and continue political, economic, and social policies contributing toward poverty, disease, and death. In medicine as in climatology, predicting hurricanes, tornadoes, and other violent weather must be secondary to ceasing pollution of land, sea, and air.

Lifelong learning humanizes work. More concretely, a process philosophy of holistic education continually rehumanizes work. Workers are fundamentally thinking human beings, human becomings, and irreducible to workers. School teaches us why and how to improve doing, and not just to do without purpose. School teaches about work. School is not the place of work. Since it teaches about work, we are human beings who are learning about what, why, and how to do ever better in production.

Thinking about work is for our and society's good. We periodically stop working and return to school in order to rehumanize our productivity. Returning to school is the academic means of becoming more whole. Becoming more whole will serve as the foundation for evolving as a more productive worker. Workers are first, last, and always human becomings. Productivity must be a holistic humanizing process.

Specialists do in order to be better human beings. Specialization is not just doing: specialists are human beings who do for human beings. Liberal arts are values guiding specialization. General education defines humanity, specialization, days off, holidays, workplace, culture. Specialization is not devoid of values. Study of specialization not devoid of values. Study is not devoid of values. Liberal arts makes explicit study of values underlying any specializaiton.

By providing non-instrumental values, philosophy is akin to lifelong learning and the process philosophy of education. Philosophers could well be the fundamental instructors in lifelong learning. Process philosophy of education becomes basic to any learning. Philosophy enables students to anticipate which jobs will be lost, which will emerge, how career fields will evolve. The philosophical attitude in process thinking involves acknowledgment of continual evolution.

Learning throughout life brings out that holistic integration. By learning continually, workers are developing their economic, social, and philosophical abilities to think ahead or feedforward, adjusting when necessary through feedback to future contingencies.

We think about doing in terms of the work-cycle by returning to (corporate and/or academic) school. Thinking enables workers to relearn basics in their career, evolving ideas and innovations changing those jobs, and learning new skills in emerging professions. Lifelong thinking about work prepares workers to meet career and work-cycle requirements before those changes occur. Bricklayers rethink traditional ways to lay bricks or rethink innovative bricklaying processes before reentering the work-cycle.

Inside the work-cycle, thinking about doing means understanding the nature, purposes, and aims of days off from going to work. In any culture, which days we allow workers to stay away from work are fundamental. Those days off influence are culture's way of reminding workers that they are human beings instead of technicians alone. Ideas about illness, rest, and productivity determine culture's future. Rethinking about days we must go to work and opportunities for staying home prepares workers to understand what will occur with the work-cycle calendar. Bricklayers continually understand why certains days are allowed off, and other days are for work.

Inside the workplace, thinking about doing involves understanding management-labor relations, worker-worker relations, and worker-client relations. What, why, and how workers do what they do at work determines productivity at the nuts-and-bolts' level. Rethinking throughout life helps workers evolve in their capabilities for improved productivity at the workplace. Bricklayers can continually understand how production is influenced by workplace practices by management, clients, co-workers, and themselves.

I would point out that even if high school and possiblly trade school beyond the secondary level are the only necessary learning required, bricklayers are human beings. They should return to school to at least relearn and rethink their skills. Bricklayers should also have some knowledge of local, national, and world events and crises that could positively or negatively influence their jobs. Every career, every area of work, however manual, is part of the network of all work from the most intellectual to the most manual.

Bricklayers cannot assume that events will not change their ideas about work. Bricklayers or other construction workers can, at some early point in their careers, find it more exciting and satisfying to try another non-intellectual job including police work, social work, office and clerical work, and so on. Our society tells persons that social mobility is possible and encouraged. Persons should never feel that once a bricklayer, always a bricklayer. The view that we remain and retire from our careers may apply to certain fields.

Medicine, law enforcement, and airline jobs can mean that experienced workers are always needed. Doctors, police, and pilots become better at their work and at thinking about their jobs. They need not feel obligated to change careers.

Physicians get to know their patients, medical innovations, and thereby serve them better. Police get to gain more experience and expertize at investigation, criminal justice, and apprehension. Commercial pilots are constantly needed for transporting large and small numbers of persons safely. Sophisticated airline equipment, unpredictable weather patterns, and innovations and changes within the aviation field make it possible and desirable for pilots to continually remain in their fields and rethink their work.

Workers' abilities to implement motions of production show competency and instrumentality. Producers must talk, listen, move their arms and legs. These physical abilities are needed for producing goods and services for ourselves and clients. We and our clients are human beings of value. All communication must take community into account. How we talk, listen, move our arms and legs, and general behave must be based on the pre- or non-instrumental values of community. Lifelong learning teaches students that as workers they must always exhibit community as the guide for communication and production.

When learning is lifelong, workers are taught that they are always communal even when they are at the workplace. Workers must always relearn the communal, social, value-oriented foundations of the economic community. Workers produce, buy, and sell as human becomings. We are never exclusively producing, buying, or selling.

Production is irreducible to transforming the environment into useful goods and services. We must develop socially desirable goods and services, and do without with minimal damage to the ecology. Selling is irreducible to conveying our products to the client in exchange for money. Buying is irreducible to taking a product and paying for it. Our values tell us that we must buy only what is good and decent for us and our loved ones. Without morals, values, and community, production would mean destroying the environment, selling would signify sales of illegal items, and buying would involve purchasing anything unethical or illegal.

Production means human beings are producing goods and services with other human beings within a social, communal context. From the perspective of life-long learning, we must continually relearn to rehumanize our actions within the workplace. How we perform by ourselves and others is part of the social dimensions of work. Going to work does not automatically result in productivity. Non-instrumental values including co-workers' feelings and needs, and clients' feelings, character, and needs are fundamental in guiding specialized or instrumental knowledge.

The value of community prevents us from reducing selling to a mechanical process. A holistic view of sales takes clients' rights into account. Federal regulations demand that poisons and other toxins for cleaning and disinfecting, and pharmaceuticals for healing, must carry warning labels. Workers are a community with clients, whether or not they see or know each other. Warning labels indicate to the buyer that harm that can come if the product is not used correctly. Companies acknowledge the holistic value of human dignity by showing customers the phone numbers that buyers may call should anything happen and help is needed.

Cleaning fluids and chemicals tell the buyer that the product is to be used only in specific locations. A product is meant to clean only the floors, another only the toilet bowl, another the bathroom sink, and another glass. Using the wrong product will at the very least not do a good job of cleaning. At most, the product will destroy the surface area. Labels and directions become very specific and precise. They indicate that users must hold the product a certain away from the body and eyes, and use only a certain amount on the area to be cleaned. Toxic items are not to be used indiscriminately as to quantity, location, temperature, or distance from the user. Workers producing these items share a human nature with their clients. Hurting clients harms workers. Society acknowledges this and says that if harm has been due to product mislabelling, clients may sue the company.

Pharmaceuticals are necessary for healing the sick. Most prescription drugs can have side-effects. Some of these side effects can be harmful and the user is given a warning to call a physician if a potentially fatal or harmful side-effect occurs. The idea of community is constant. Workers learn throughout life that community,values, and human dignity guide production and distribution from the workplace.

The notion of the prescription tells us that some drugs are over-the-counter, while other drugs require physician request. Over-the-counter drugs are produced with care, and dispensed with warning labels. Prescription drugs are produced with similar care, but dispensed only when the physician asks the pharmacist to make it available to the buyer. The buyer should not be able to purchase a prescription drug at will. Such a purchase could provide the buyer with a product that can harm the patient.

Clothing is similar. We buy and wear clothing whether or not our health is good. Clothing manufacturers tell us on labels how we are to clean the articles. Labels indicate the need for dry-clearning, and the water temperture and kind of detergent. Workers do not just sell us a product without informing us of the proper care and cleaning of those goods.

If the workplace were reducible to making money, products would come without labels about cleaning and care. Without warnings and information, buyers might well clean and care for the product incorrectly, and the product would be spoiled or damaged beyond repair. From the purely materialistic point of view of inert ideas, buyers would then need to buy another product of the same kind to replace the one damaged, and workers make more money.

Fortunately, government regulations requiring labels about care can prevent materialism. Workers are told to be a community with buyers by warning the buyers about care and cleaning. Buyers purchase products as needed or desired. Purchases are not done to replace items that the purchaser unintentionally destroyed due to ignorance of proper care.

Workers who produce clothing that ignites under hot temperatures are doing something illegal. The government warns manufacturers of producing article of clothing that can catch fire and kill or seriously burn the wearer.

Society is always learning that childrens' toys must be physically safe. Our values are being exhibited as society debates whether children should be given safe toy guns and rifles.

Workers at the workplace may not produce items for the sake of profit. Authors who write books denying the Holocaust do a major disservice to themselves as well as offending the Jewish community. These authors eventually deny that the American military encountered terrible Nazi deeds inEurope'. In denying what occurred to the Jews, authors who deny the Holocaust deny the terror that hit so many millions of non-Jews.

Every workplace is more than an economic location. Workplaces are irreducible to economics, paychecks, and production. Each place of work is a minimal community. As workers work and relate to each other and clients, a minimal sense of community unfolds because workers and clients are irreducible to mechanical production and physiology of consumption. Holistic, developing human beings orhuman becomings with dignity work as part of communal existence, and are irreducible to doing.

Following Alfred North Whitehead's idea of inert ideas,[17]Alfred North Whitehead' says philosophy is the critique of abstractions.[18] Abstractions mean analyzing experience into parts in order to understand the whole. Philosophy knows abstracting is necessary, but also knows that we must critique the abstractions by putting them into integrated, evolving perspective connected with all other abstractions of partial views of the whole. My present chapter as a process philosophy of lifelong learning is a critique of abstract motions within specialized study.

Alfred North Whitehead warns against inert ideas. My present chapter criticizes inert specialized motions. Reducing motions in specialized study to unthinking mechanization is inert motion. Students need to think about motions in their professions.

4. Preventing Starvation

What does a student mean in criticizing Hutchins by saying that we would starve to death we did what he advocates? Those who criticize Robert Maynard Hutchins emphasis on thinking, say that we should only learn how to work. I argue that a look at specialized study shows are more fundamental thought.

Doing things that should not be done in a technical sense results in the company going down and people "starving" by losing their jobs. Thinking about doing enables people to do only what is technically and ethically correct. In the long run, thinking about doing avoids legal and ethical pitfalls.

Sociologist of work, Fred Davis, would argue that the workplace is irreducible to motions and techniques. All movements in our daily work must be within a context of evolving values, and the holistic ideas of human beings. Work motions become "crass" when jobs are reducible to technique and devoid of values.

Jack Blaeser was not asking people to simply do more. His advice was that they always question what and why they are doing. Concord employees would starve by losing their jobs as the company closes due to their continuing to do things which are unproductive or meaningless. They do not starve when they always take time out to think about and improve what they are doing.

Workers do not starve by thinking about doing. They starve by doing without thinking, and thinking without doing. Corporations need the holistic view of aim, purpose, direction, and humanity. No business can survive for long if its employees do not feel that they count. For workers to only perform mechanically and never think about what and why they are doing as they do, relegates them to the status of machines and slavery.

In any discipline and vocation, workers must be encouraged to think about what they are doing, and do what they think is best. To do without thinking reduces them to dehumanized objects. To think without doing means that they can think and come up with good ideas about performance and productivity. Thinking without doing is as hazardous and thinking without knowing data. Nothing stands in isolation from reality. Reality involves thinking, knowing, and doing. The holistic approach to disciplinary activity integrates thinking with doing. Failure to integrate doing within thinking reduces doing to inert ideas.

Seven

REHUMANIZING DATA

Inside thinking about doing, theory is lifelong relative to data. Theory never stops. We always theorize. Collecting and evaluating data manifests the theory that we can gather perceive and experience.

Data does not stand without theory. Data without theory means inert ideas. Students are human beings who require theory as the basis for experience, observation, or data. Theory humanizes data. Evolving, theorizing human beings study data. Theory orients and provides non-instrumental value to the instrumentality of data.

1. The Theory-Data Continuum

In Chapter Four, I mentioned that we must always resimplify the information explosion. The explosion of data and theory must be continually reorganized into a more general theory. Inside the reorganization, data is continuous with theory.

At the Fall of the Middle Ages, objectivity instead of Church authority needed to be the basis of knowledge. Scholars understood that their own thinking, and in the case of science, instruments, comprised the tools for knowledge and the search for truth. Thinking and theorizing allows us to develop the holistic context to understand data. Instruments are the means of gathering that data.

Observation and the collection of data is not independent of the theory behind it. Seeing, touching, smelling, and otherwise gathering information assumes that we can accumulate data. Data or observation do occur in isolation from thought. From the perspective of lifelong learning, we always acquire data, and must understand that a theory is always at work behind our acquisition of data.

From the perspective of Alfred North Whitehead, theory and data are a continuum. Theory is lifelong as is data. Alfred North Whitehead rarely uses the word theory. He uses the terms general ideas,[1] generality,[2] and principles.[3] His inclination to use the words ideas, generality, and so on, is irrelevant. Underlying his terminology is the intention to say that data requires a holistic context in which to make sense.

Alfred North Whitehead calls inert data that kind of information devoid of theory. He says we do not fill students with data as we would pack articles in a trunck. Carrying that forward, we do not seek facts as though they exist independent of a theory. I would argue that lifelong theory protects us from inert data. Theory provides the cognitive and humane perspective in which data makes sense. The mind is not a passive entity for the mere collection of data.[4]

Lifelong learning is supported again with Alfred North Whitehead's view of imagination or theory. Theory is a "living"[5] process continuing throughout life, and never put into the mind once and for all complete as a collection of data. We never memorize a theory. Theories reduced to memorization become stagnant. Students and teachers must continually think about, discuss, and debate theory.

In education as in scientific work, theorizing and observation go hand-in-hand. Theory without observation ignores the real world; observation without theory is meaningless and perhaps impossible.[6] Observation without theory comprises inert ideas or as I call them, inert observations. People cannot perceive discreet entities.

Data is one aspect of school and learning. The educational system demands something more in order to make sense of learning and data: theory and living dialogue. Alfred North Whitehead knows the need for general ideas or pinciples.

Karl Popper would be another excellent supporter for lifelong theory as against inert ideas. He presents a powerful story about the need for acknowledging theory as the basis for observation. Popper once asked students to write down their observations. Students asked him what he wished them to observe. We never merely "observe." We observe and gather data about something.[7] That "something" involves the theoretical orientation of our perceptions. Cold, directionless, totally objective or external observations or data do not exist.

The field of astrophysics provides a good example of the theory-data continuum. Scientists typically develop a theory and then see if data fits into the theory. They modify or reject theory as data comes in. Typical research assumes that data is data, and needs no further exploration. Data either fits or does not fit into the proposed theory.

Vincent Kiernan[8] points out that improved software now allows astrophysicists to experiment differently. Astrophysicists propose a theory and collect data to see if the data fits the theory. In collecting the information, they do not just look at the data as a collection of patternless, context-free entities concuring with or contradicting the theory. Even if data fits into the theory which began the search, astrophysicists now see more in the data. Subjecting the data to innovative software, they search the data to see if it contains unknown patterns and wholes.

Data is not just dry, cold bits and pieces of explicit information from the stars, planets, asteroids, galaxies, and so on. We cannot insist that information is an either/or situation, either substantiating or dumping a theory about the universe or a set of phenomena. Information may or may not substantiate a given theory. Data is more than what our eyes and instruments perceive. The holistic view means that information may contain as yet unknown patterns which will shed further light on research.

Distance can determine the truths in data. The farther we are from astrophysical events such as collapsing and colliding galaxies, the more we need to investigate the data we perceive. Complex astrophysical activity that occurs billions of light years ago requires complex ways of analyzing the data it generates. If we are not relatively near the events, we cannot see what is occurring. The farther away we are from the events, the more subtle become the data and patterns reaching us. We need to interpret and analyze the information in ever more sophisticated ways.

If Karl Popper had the luxury of contemporary astrophysics and computer science, he would tell his students more than the need for theory. He would have told them the need for more complex ways of looking at the theories and analyzing the information. If his students were asked today to observe, they would have answered a more sophisticated question. Karl Popper's students asked what it was that he wanted them to observe. If he had asked them to observe astrophysical data in 1999, they would have asked him a deeper question. His students would have wanted to know which aspect of the observation they should consider. Karl Popper's students would want to know if they should observe the data initially coming in, or the results being generated by a computer dissecting this data for the more subtle information. Lifelong theory means that data we perceive is always a matter of interpretation.

I turn to another example of the need for lifelong theory from astrophysics. Until 1965 astrophysicists were unable to observe radio waves at certain levels of radiation from the universe. These waves would be from the first moments of the Big Bang and would be evidence of some kind of major Bang creating the universe. The astrophysicists were theorizing that such radio waves could not exist at certain levels. Their theory meant that they would not look for such waves at levels at which they had been observing. Theory tells us what to observe.

In the astrphysicists' case, they happened to notice a strange set of radiation coming from the universe.[9] Their theory denied that background noise from the Big Bang could exist at the level of observation for which they had set their equipment. Astrophysicists repeatedly tried fixing their equipment in the belief that mechanical problems created this strange noise. The noise persisted. Eventually, conversations with an MIT professor convinced the astrophysicists that the noise observed at the present levels was what they were seeking. The initial theory that no noise could exist that the original levels of radiation, was changed. Theory may be wrong, but is always the major and initial context telling us how to observe.

We do not just observe and then build a theory. Our theories come before, guide, and orient what we observe. Astrophysicists did not build their theory about the nonexistence of noise at certain levels by hearing or not hearing noise. They assumed that the noise for which they would be listening could not exist at certain levels. Astrophysicists did not build the theory by first listening, hearing nothing, and then deciding that noise could not exist that those levels. Their theory came first and was based on speculation. So strong are theories that we may challenge the evidence when they contradict those theories. Astrophysicists checked and double-checked their instruments before finally concluding that noise exists at certain levels. We need to always interpret our observations and data. Interpretations can be seen during war as well as peace.

I bring up the example of misinformation. Information or data is considered truthful. We see information suggesting that a galaxy is colliding with another galaxy, or that a star is imploding or exploding. Natural does not lie. Human beings can and do lie. They often do so for the sake of survival in wartime. An enemy who wishes to destroy the innocent will give out erroneous or misinformation. The aim is to fool the innocent as to the enemy's strength, troop movements, weapons, and so on. The innocent nation or nations need also to misinform the enemy. Innocent nations need to fool the enemy to think that an attack will take place in one place, in order to have the enemy move its forces to defend that location. The innocent nation's aim is to weaken the enemy's forces defending the location of the actual attack.

We have the admonition to read between the lines. Lines may be literally lines of words, or the words. Words can mean that the speaker or writer is lying to us. We should read between the lines as well as the lines. Reading between the lines means that as we read the words, we must vigilantly ask ourselves what they mean, and what does the writer think in writing these words. Readers should never accept everything at face value.

Information or data is not just what we perceive. What do we observe during war? We observe military equipment moving to a certain location. That equipment may be sufficiently large or made of inflated rubber to give the enemy the idea that a nation's military is preparing for defensive or offensive activity in a given location. A government performing such movement is attempting to divert the enemy to think a certain military operation will occur.

If the innocent or enemy government looks only at the information, they are fooled and foolish. That government looks at such information only as inert ideas. A government may feel that it needs to analyze and consider the facts, data, or information generated by other governments. A government needs spies within the enemy camp. A government needs reliable spies who will provide accurate information to their country. Dependable spies give accurate information. Double agents give false information to one country and true information to another.

John Mesenbrink tells of previously classified U.S. military satellite information now available those willing to pay for the data.[10] In the worst case scenario, terrorists and enemy agents can buy our previously top secret information. In the best case scenario, corporation executives can buy reliable information about competitors in different parts of the world. Buying data about the competitor sounds like a dream come true. CEOs want valuable data available until now only to the government's highest military and civilian echelon dealing with the most sensitive aspects of national security.

CEOs cannot be trusted to take data and do well with it. The aims, ends, purposes, or values directing the data they purchase will result in corporate success or failure. Theoretical and contextual direction fleshed out with data, not just a collection of information, determine the future of CEOs and corporations. Data lacking aims, purposes, or values become inert ideas.

Let me consider the meaning of government agencies during peace or war. Government agencies are not just governmental organizations. Let me note the idea of agencies that do investigations. Any government agency investigates. Probing is a daily event. We probe for records, for information not yet in files, employers ask employees and recruit for information. Saying that agencies probe is insufficent. In terms of identity, some agencies investigate crimes while others probe the causes of disease.

The Federal Bureau of Investigation (FBI), the United State Secret Service, Drug Enforcement Administration (DEA), and Bureau of Alchohol, Tobacco, and Firearms (ATF) all investigate crime. Each probes a different category of crime, though sometimes these overlap. FBI goes after kidnappers, spies, bank robbers, serial killers, and certain other criminals committing federal crimes. Secret Service agents guard the president and go after counterfeiters. DEA investigates drug pushers, and ATF searches for violations of alcohol, tobacco, and guns, although it has also joined in searches for terrorists and others planting bombs. Federal agents go after criminals who violate federal laws. State police search for criminals violating state laws, and local police seek those who violate city ordinances.

The Center for Disease Control investigates diseases. If employees of any of these agencies were to indicate to strangers that the employees work, the question would be "what kind of work?" People do not just "work." If the answer was that the employees investigate, the next question would be "investigate what?" We do not just work, and do not simply investigate. Employees investigate crimes, diseases, and other specific categories. Even if the government decided on one federal bureau to investigate crime, that agency would still be investigating crime and not disease.

Speaking of crime, take the idea of criminal profiling. Retired FBI agent, John Douglas, writes about the profiling of criminals.[11] We have two extremes in law enforcement. One extreme is to only seek the facts. This extreme is the traditional law enforcement approach, where police ask many routine questions about the incident, who saw what, when, and so on. The other extreme is prejudice: certain races commit crimes. Scientific profiling is between these two extremes. Law enforcement officials study the personality types who commit certain crimes. When approaching a crime scene, police are to ask what kind of man or woman would do this thing?

Recent events[12] where police have arrested suspects due to race show that we can confuse scientific profiling with prejudice. Scientific profiling involves years of study by law enforcement I just mentioned. Racial profiling is not scientific profiling. Racial profiling is prejudice. Some law officers do what people in any job do. They believe from the start that certain races, ethnic groups, religions, and so on, are criminals.

When a crime occurs, investigators do not just ask questions about who saw what. The investigators also do not excercise bias. They attempt to determine the kind of person who would commit a crime. Their investigation follows a profile of a personality and does not just rest on asking what witnesses saw. Scientific profiling is the correct way, and bias a distortion of, people behaving according to theories and ideas instead of theories reducible to facts.

At MIT, scholars theorize in order to understand the world, and data.[13] MIT proudly states that its professors are engaged in activity ranging from the most practical aspects of problem-solving, to the most theoretical foundations of knowledge. The ability to solve existing problems is necessary. Society needs people who can determine a resolve as many issues as possible. Civilization also needs learned people to understand why these problems exist, why and how to solve them in humane ways, and how serious problems may be prevented in the future.

I find it telling that among the most prestigious thinkers in modern times are theoretical physicists. Albert Einstein spent his time with pencil and paper to develop ideas concerning physics. From the perspective of Alfred North Whitehead, imagination and theory need facts upon which to build. He argues that just as important, we must develop a theoretical vision of the world that underlies and gives meaning to those facts. Foolishness takes theory or imagination without facts; the pedant looks at facts devoid of theory and imagination.[14]

Huston C. Smith speaks about the ongoing need for theory to explain data.[15] Ironically, he has written on education as well. No fact without theory, says Huston C. Smith. Every fact or piece of data express a theory behind it. At the least, data reveals the theory that data exists. At the most, data reveals the theory we may later discover or existing theory we may modify concerning the data.

John Clarke[16] says that concepts and theories give meaning to data. We do not start with value-free, theory-free data or 'inert ideas' and then hunt for their theoretical context. Concepts and theories give us the direction, purpose, and meaning of any data. Scholars working with data assume that data exists. Assumptions are very broad theoretical and value contexts. Scholars may gather data about violence in schools. These thinkers are not just putting down numbers and words on paper. Their projects begin with the believe that violent behavior is being exhibited in schools.

The idea of the calendar is a popular reminder of the idea of theory underlying data. We do not just have numbered days: we call them Monday, Tuesday, etc., according to cultural names. Months are also called by cultural names: January, February, and so on, instead month one, two, and three. Days go by, and are marked by holidays or holy days. Time is not simply a collection of days or months. The calendar is centered around wholes in terms of holidays, and cultural names for days and months.

2. Inert Ideas

The traditional educational system thrives on memorization of facts. Alfred North Whitehead criticizes traditional education for telling students to simply memorize data. He calls "inert ideas"[17] the method and content of data to be memorized without allowing student participation. Forcing students to memorize facts without understanding those facts is akin to compelling the students to move like robots without understanding why they move. People are irreducible to anatomy. They do not just push, pull, walk, speak, or perform other functions. They are human beings, doing things within purpose.

The same should be said of data and theory. Minds are not meant to just perceive data. Mere perception of data is cognitive robotics. Persons would be forced to simply know without understanding, just as robots move without knowing why they move.

To insist that we must feed students with data devoid of theory is a contradiction. Feeding them data, or, as Alfred North Whitehead puts it, packing them with facts as we would article in a trunk, expresses the theory that we must pack students with data. Ask teachers why they feed students with data to memorize, and they will tell you that knowledge and wisdom result from feeding students with data. Such a reply assumes the theory that we know only because we are feed data.

What is data? What are the facts? Ask liberals and conservatives to support their opposing views, and they will indicate their ideas or theories instead of giving you the "facts." Liberals indicate that we need adequate government to help every person. Adequate government is not data. Governmental responsibility or the government's role is a theory. Conservatives argue that the less government and more personal responsibility we have the better. Each group is spelling out its theory of life and not a collection of data.

Ask liberals to give you the facts, and they will show you that people are happy when feed, clothed, healed, and so on, even if by the government. Conservatives argue that government makes people lazy. Each group can probably find sufficient data to support its claims.

Should nuclear power plants exist? The facts are that Three Mile Island had a near disaster. What caused that problem? Bad training of technicians? Poor design? If we decide to continue building such reactors, we are deciding on the theory that catastrophy is unlikely, and that we need these reactors. If we decide to discontinue building them due to what occurred at Three Mile Island, we are interpreting the data to mean that the accident was not catastrophic. What of Chernobyl? People may believe that while the Russian disaster was overwhelming, we still need reactors and should not discontinue with those existing.

The feminist movement has done much to show the need for theory. Feminism has sought to deny that observation is free of values and theory. Feminists argue that knowledge has traditionally been a male domain. Women writers maintain that men have established scientific and humanistic goals which would be different if women had had more power to do so.

Read history books and you typically find men as the leading if not the only scholars. These seem to be the facts. The fact seems to be that men alone think, and that women have no place in intellectual or other history. The fact that women have also made contributions in intellectual and other history suggests that the traditional data was colored by males, and the newer ones colored by females. We were not traditionally being given the whole truth about who contributed to knowledge. Society is never producing purely cognitive information.

2. Inert Theory

We can wrongly believe that observation is neutral and never need theory. Can we have inert theories? I would argue that naive theory is possible. Theory is lifelong and requires data. Theory and data are a continuum. Theory that is alone is as inadequate as data that is alone.

Lifelong theory means only that theory is as lifelong as data. Data is always theory-oriented. Lifelong theory does not imply theory without data.

MIT lauds researchers who deal with the remotest reaches of theory.[18] Theoreticians establish intellectual and other goals. They provide the groundwork for further research. Theoreticians are thinking about the most logical, reasonable, possible ways in which reality occurs. Given certain rules, they attempt to dicipher the implications and potentialities of those theories. Theoreticians know that they need data.

Theoreticians who ignore data and the results of experiments are fooling themselves. Economic, physical, chemical, social, and other theories are important in attempting to determine how and why we do as we do. In each case, a refusal to consider experimentation, data, retheorizing, modifying our ideas, and so on, results in a theoretical solipsism. We become isolated from the world. Theory means wholeness, and wholeness includes the parts we call data.

Richard Wilk[19] warns that theory, while giving meaning to cannot be divorced from data. Unrealistic theory is as bad as data without theory is impossible. To develop a theory without seeking some grounding in data is akin to assuming that what we perceive is the truth. Theory must be developed with an eye toward its modification and change.

Theory always exists with data. Lifelong learning means that we must always assume and seek theory as we study data. Theory is irreducible to data, and we must always study data in terms of the wholeness of theory. Holistic theory and data overcome inert ideas as mutually exclusive theories and data.

Eight

CONCLUSION

My previous seven chapters reveal the wholes and values underlying lifelong learning which prevent inert ideas. I conclude my book with the present chapter putting into focus the dangers of inert ideas.

A society believing in inert ideas falls into a backward state of chaos and dehumanization. We no longer understand reality, each other, or ourselves. People behave without thinking, and can get killed or injured everyday due to improper environments and designs. What appears to be scholarship eventully fails to result in holistic knowledge and values, and leads toward pedants hating and attempting to harm each other. An educational system clogged with inert ideas no longer educates human becomings. The educational system filled with inert ideas produces passive students behaving like robots. These students will become passive, robotic workers.

1. Inert Ideas of Traditional Education

In traditional education, learning and work are inert ideas. Learning starts with kindergarden and ends at graduation. After graduation, students become workers and no longer learn.

The consequences of traditional learning as inert ideas are serious for society. Workers never return to school to relearn basic ideas. As a result, workers forget much of what the formal educational system teaches them. Learning is once-for-all. Courses which relate to jobs are implemented as students join the workforce. Any material which is not directly job-related is lost to the memory. Teaching and learning become a waste of time when teachers teach material that will never be relearned. Unless workers need history, biology, reading and writing, geography, and other courses throughout their lives, these courses are forgotten and their benefit lost.

Inert ideas during work involve a static society. Workers only work. We see no innovations in medicine and health, law and ethics, a better understanding of the world and universe. Workers only go to work, produce, consume, and eventually retire and die.

The ecological implications of inert ideas are immense. Production and consumption involve discarding of waste and used or obsolete products. Senseless discarding creates the throw-away society, a society which uses things briefly and throws them away. Garbage is thrown away without thinking about its environmental consequences. The nation and world soon become a junk yard when discarded goods reflect inert ideas instead of aspects of recycling.

Students learning inert ideas are passive students when in the classroom, and passive workers after graduation. Passive workers are robots working without thinking and learning. Passive workers become passive citizens.

2. Inert Ideas in Distance Learning

Consider inert ideas in distance learning. Distance learning in school involves inert ideas if interaction between students and teachers does not occur. Without interactive distance learning, even lifelong learning suffers. Distance learning without interaction reduces education to the inert ideas of passive learning. Students may attend schools throughout life, but the lack of interaction means passive learning lacking creativity and dignity.

Passive students become a problem for society. These students become workers who will never innovate and progress. Even if workers return to school in lifelong learning, their education is never progressive if the learning is passive. Workers can return to school to learn new ideas, but these are given to them in lectures where students lack the opportunity to interrelate with instructors. Distance learning and lifelong learning lose their innovative potentials and degenerate into inert ideas when passive listening is the only means of learning even throughout life.

3. Inert Ideas in Interactive Distance Learning

Interactive distance learning, whether in traditional or lifelong learning, can mean inert ideas if technology replaces classrooms. Students become dependent on mediate, technological means of learning.

Inert ideas reduce learning and interaction to speaking into microphones, viewing students and teachers on monitors, and being recognized only as others view you on their monitors and look into their cameras. Social interaction and immediacy are replaced by electronic devices.

Whatever the advantages of interactive distance learning, electronic means must always be incorporated within an educational system putting classrooms at the center of learning. People are not sights, sounds, hands, and voices. People are human beings, human becomings, giving meaning to anatomy, neurology, voice, and other biological dimensions.

Teaching students and workers that electronic methods are the primary or only means of lifelong learning, defeats the idea of ongoing education. Ongoing education must involve the holistic approach to human beings, and overcome the inert ideas of reducing students to interrelate only electronically even in lifelong learning.

4. Inert Ideas in the Information Explosion

The information explosion can be a devastating example of inert ideas. A growing amount of data and theory without a simplifying and reorganizing theory means vast quantities of obsolete and chaotic material. Ongoing reorganization can put increasing volumes of data into more structured wholes.

Our biggest libraries are reduced to the inert ideas of meaningless and irrelevant books and articles. Scholars can create specialties and subspecialties which never relate to each other. Communication among specialists and subspecialists stops. Efforts to understand the physical universe as a unity can be seriously undermined with the inert ideas that major differing theories of the world are inherently incompatible. Efforts to understand the social sciences and humanities are in trouble as inert ideas tell us that arts and sciences are fundamentally unrelated.

Specialists and subspecialists infected with inert ideas write books and articles as though their differing fields are completely distinct from each other. Publications would say that the specialties and subspecialties never relate and are inherent isolated from each other.

Inert ideas in traditional education mean that we cram unrelated data into passive students before graduation. Inert ideas in the information explosion and lifelong learning do not denote the automatically positive. Specialists and subspecialists publishing their findings in isolated fields fill students and workers with more and more unrelated data. Returning to school to learn the latest research does no good if findings are unrelated to each other, and the latest theories and data are devoid of more general frameworks.

5. Inert Ideas and Liberal Arts

The liberal arts and specialization can suffer in terms of inert ideas. If inert ideas in the information explosion mean subspecialists in a given specialty do not communicate with each other or with subspecialists in other disciplines, inert ideas in the liberal arts would more broadly result in specialists in arts and sciences failing to interrelate.

Specialists and subspecialists reflecting inert ideas reduce themselves to isolated, passive disciplinarians lacking cognitive coherence and personal qualities. Scholars and all professionals yell and scream at each other if and when they communicate. They fail to respect fellow human beings and society declines as an interacting whole. Yelling and screaming workers can bring down careers and seriously damage companies.

Lifelong learning of specialization without the liberal arts reduces the study of specialization to inert ideas. If workers return to school only to learn about becoming more competent technicians, families and communities suffer. Specialization without values, families, and neighborhoods result in family and community breakdown. Inert ideas of people reduced to specialists ignoring life outside work undermines the glue of wholes and values keeping society, families, and communities together. Lifelong learning must be based on human becoming as a holistic enterprise irreducible to specialized, cognitive, or technical expertize.

6. Inert Ideas in Disciplinary Motions

Inert ideas in disciplinary motions involves doing without thinking. When people do thoughtlessly, they behave in unsafe manners. Procedures, organizations, and technology require constant attention for efficient and safe productivity.

With inert ideas replacing thinking about what we do, people would simply do and perhaps get killed or seriously injured at work, home, and all other places. Motions and objects in the physical environment are irreducible to discreet movements and entities the sum total of which means productivity. Productivity requires a holistic approach to see how to improve what we do and where we work. Injuries, medical bills, absenteeism, and other facets of unsafe and unsatisfactory workplaces will destroy the economy and society.

The emphasis on ergonomics in the workplace tells us to face the issue of thinking about motions. Thinking about motions puts motions and procedures into their holistic perspective avoiding reduction of technique to inert ideas.

Inert ideas in disciplinary motions reduce students and workers to robots. Students passively, robotically do as they are taught without thinking about what they are doing. Workers passively, robotically do as they are told without thinking about their actions and procedures.

7. Inert Ideas in Theory and Data

Motions are part of a coherent whole. Data is also part of a coherent unity. If we do not just do, we also do not just know data.

Inert ideas in motions can result in people doing things that get them injured or killed. Inert ideas in data will result in people reading numbers and words without understanding the total picture. Inert ideas in movement reduce people to robots. Inert ideas in cognition reduce human beings to receptacles of data.

Data can mean different things according to different theories and scenarios. Refusal to acknowledge that view involves the inert ideas resulting in a lack of understanding and appreciating the world around us. Knowledge and intellectual progress depend on theoretical constructs giving direction to data. Data devoid of theoretical context means inert ideas whereby people are helpless to orient themselves toward the future.

Passive students become pedants who memorize without ever thinking. After graduation they become passive workers who memorize workplace data without thinking about work.

8. Inert Ideas and Global Disaster

If we reduce learning and work to the inert ideas of complete education followed by lifelong work, society falls backward. If lifelong learning involves the inert ideas of passive distant learning or interactive distant learning replacing classrooms, workers become tools of technology. Inert ideas of incoherent and obsolete amounts of information result in worthless knowledge. Inert ideas of specialization without liberal arts, technicians lacking values, arts and sciences devoid of unity, and science ignoring the humanities, lead to a world of technical experts who could bring about another Holocaust or destroy ecology.

Inert ideas involving disciplinary doing devoid of thought, and data without theoretical context, reduce human behavior to mechanization and literacy to memorizing statistics.

In the end, inert ideas lead to social dissolution and ecological destruction. Only wholeness and values overcome inert ideas and dehumanization. Without a lifelong commitment to social and ecological wholes continually checking and correcting inert ideas, humanity faces annihilation.

The dangers of inert ideas touch on all aspects of human existence. Ecological and social ills comprise some of the crises. Nuclear and biochemical wars, especially an accidental launching of missiles, are other catastrophies. Leaders who put nuclear and germ warfare arsenals above the need to push for global disarmement and the search for peace, are engaging in inert ideas of national security. Nuclear reactors experiencing accidents can also mean mass destruction. Even safe nuclear reactors can represent inert ideas of energy when storage difficulties of decaying radioactive materials edges toward ecological doom. The aim of a process philosophy of education is lifelong wholes promoting families, environment, community, and civilization. Lifelong education means unending vigilance against reducing humanity to passive, robotic inert ideas.

NOTES

Introduction

1. Alfred North Whitehead, *The Aims of Education* (New York: Mentor, 1964), p. xi.

ONE: Rehumanizing Work

1. Fred Davis, "The Cabdriver and His Fare," *The Social Dimensions of Work*, ed. Clifton D. Bryant (Englewood Cliffs, N.J.: Prentice- Hall, 1972) p. 408.

2. *THIS IS MIT, MASSACHUSETTS INSTITUTE OF TECHNOLOGY CATALOGUE, 1961-1962 BULLETIN*, p. 6.

3. *Ibid.*, p. 50.

4. Henry Winthrop, "Generalists and Specialists," *The Journal of Higher Education*, 37:4 (April 1966), p. 200.

5. Reiko Yamada, "Higher Education Reform: Toward a Lifelong Learning Society," *CAEL Forum and News*, 23:1 (Fall 1999), p. 13.

6. Alfred North Whitehead, *The Aims of Education* (New York: Mentor, 1964), p. 46.

7. Edward B. Fiske, "Booming Corporate Education Rivals College Programs, Study Says," *The New York Times*, 34:46,303 (26 January 1985), p. 9.

8. R. L. Jones, "Beyond School Walls," *Action in Teacher Education*, 4:4 (1982), p. 1.

9. Russell V. Gerbman, "Corporate Universities 101," *HR Magazine*, 45:2 (February 2000), p. 102

10. *Ibid.*

11. Alfred North Whitehead, *Science and the Modern World* (New York: Mentor; 1964), p. 176.

12. *Ibid.*

13. Ernest L. Boyer, "Changing Dimensions in Higher Education," *The College Board Review*, no. 87 (Spring 1973), p. 19.

14. John W. Gardner, "Agenda for the Colleges and Universities," *Campus 1980*, ed. Alvin Eurich (New York: Dell Publishing Company, Inc., 1968), p. 4.

15. Alfred North Whitehead, *The Aims of Education*, p. xl.

16. *Ibid.*

17. David Bevington, ed. *The Complete Works of William Shakespeare* (New York: Longman, 1997), p. 1077.

18. Ernest L. Boyer, "Changing Dimensions in Higher Education," p. 20.

19. Alfred North Whitehead, *Science and The Modern World*, p. 175.

20. *Ibid.*

21. Mircea Eliade, *Myth and Reality* (New York: Harper Torchbooks, 1963), p. 7.

22. *Ibid.*

23. *Ibid.*

24. Roger Brown, "From Codability to Coding Ability," *Learning About Learning*, ed. Jerome S. Bruner (Washington: U. S. Government Printing Office; 1966), p. 188.

25. Robert Maynard Hutchins, *The Learning Society* (New York: Mentor, 1966), p. 13.

26. Robert Maynard Hutchins, *The Conflict of Education in Democratic Society* (New

York: Harper & Row, 1953), p. 76.

27. *Ibid.*

28. David W. Neubauer, *America's Courts and the Criminal Justice System,* 5th Edition (Belmont, Cal.: Wadsworth Publishing Company, 1996), p. x.

29. Carl E. Lutrin and Allen K. Settle, *American Public Administration: Concepts & Cases,* 2nd Edition (San Luis Opispo, Cal.: Mayfield Publishing Company, 1976), p.xiii.

30. Norbert Wiener, *Cybernetics* (Cambridge, Mass.: The MIT Press, 1961), p. i.

31. Richard A. Johnson, Fremont E. Kast, and James A. Rosenzweig, *The Theory and Management of Systems,* Third Edition (New York: McGraw-Hill Book Company, 1973), p. xi.

32. Ludwig Wittgenstein, *Tractatus Logico-Philosophicus* (London: Routledge & Kegan Paul, 1961), p. 5.

33. Ludwig Wittgenstein, *Philosophical Investigations* (New York: Macmillan, 1958), p. 21.

34. David Barnum, *The Supreme Court & American Democracy* (New York: St. Martin's, 1993), p. 313.

35. Norman Perrin, *Jesus and the Language of the Kingdom* (Philadelphia: Fortress Press, 1976), p. xi.

36. A.A. Liveright, "Learning Never Ends: A Plan for Continuing Education," *Campus 1980,* ed. Alvin C. Eurich (New York: Dell Publishing Company, 1968), p. 150.

37. Rosalind Rossi, "Daley invites parents to first day of school," *Chicago Sun-Times* (19 August 2000), p. 1.

TWO: Rehumanizing Distance Learning

1. Alfred North Whitehead, *The Aims of Education* (New York: Mentor, 1958), p. i.

2. Paulo Freire, *Pedagogy of the Oppressed,* Trans. Myra Bergman Ramos (New York: Continuum, 1992), ch. 2.

3. Martin Buber, *I and Thou* (New York: Charles Scribner, 1970), p. 53.

4. Martha W. Thomas, "Business Communication in the Modern Age," *Business & Economic Review,* 44:4 (July-Aug-September 1998), p. 20.

THREE: Rehumanizing Educational Location

1. Bettina Fabos and Michelle D. Young, "Telecommunication in the Classroom," *Review of Educational Research,* 69:3 (Fall 1999), p. 250.

2. Kelly Mccollom, "A Computer Requirement for students Changes Professors' Duties As Well," *The Chronicle of Higher Education,* 44:42 (26 June 1998), p. A22.

3. Fred Davis, "The Cabdriver and His Fare," *The Social Dimensions of Work,* ed. Clifton D. Bryant (Englewood Cliffs, N.J.: Prentice-Hall, 1962), p. 428.

FOUR: Rehumanizing the Information Explosion

1. Mark Donald Bowles, *Crisis in the Information Age?* (Ann Arbor, Mich.: University Microfilms, Inc., 1999), p. iii.

2. Alfred North Whitehead, *The Aims of Education* (New York: Mentor, 1964), p. 36.

3. Alfred North Whitehead, *Symbolism* (New York: Capricorn, 1927), p. 61.

4. *Ibid.*, p. 37.

5. Richard E. Bellman, "Dynamic Programming, Intelligent Machines, and Self-Organizing System," *Symposium on the Mathematical Theory of Automata, Polytechnic Institute of Brooklyn* (24, 25, 26 April 1962), p. 2.

6. *Ibid.*

7. James J. Doherty, "A Few Suggestions for Handling Criminal Appeals," *Case & Comment*, 75:1 (January-February 1970), p. 35.

8. Alfred North Whitehead, *The Aims of Education*, p. 22.

9. *Ibid.*, p. 94.

10. Richard E. Bellman, "Dynamic Programming, Intelligent Machines, and Self-Organizing Systems," p. 4.

11. Mariam Rodin, Karen Michaelson and Gerald M. Britan, "Systems Theory in Anthropology," *Current Anthropology*, 10:4. (December 1978), p. 750.

12. *Ibid.*

13. *Ibid.*

14. Manfred Clynes, "Toward a View of Man," *Biomedical Engineering Systems*, ed. Manfred Clynes and J. H. Milsum (New York: McGraw-Hill, 1970), p. 272.

15. Russell L. Ackoff, "Systems, Organizations, and Interdisciplinary Research," *Yearbook of the Society for General System Theory*, vol. 6 (1961), p. 1.

16. Lisa Rabasca, "Mischel sees Psychological Review as forum to connect with new fields," *Monitor*, 31:1 (January 2000), p. 82.

17. George Waltz, "Thinking Ahead With Vannevar Bush," *International Science and Technology*, Prototype Issue (January 1961), p. 55.

18. *Webster's Third International Dictionary*. Springfield, Mass.: Merriam-Webster, 1993, p.108.

19. Michael M. Kazanjian, "Theology of Culture: Some Aspects of the Sacred Dimensions of the Secular," *Delta Epsilon Sigma Bulletin*, 16:1 (March 1971), p. 21.

20. Julian Pitt-Rivers, *The Fate of Shechem, or the Politics of Sex* (London: Cambridge University Press, 1977), p. 130.

21. *Ibid.*

22. Jerome Hall, "Perennial Problems of Criminal Law," *The Hofstra Law Review*. 1:1. (Spring 1973), p. 31.

23. George Blondin and David Green, "A Unifying Model of Bioenergetics," *Chemical & Engineering News*, 53:20 (10 November 1975), p. 26.

24. Mike Lobash, "Two Codes, Too Bad: A failed attempt to create a national fire code leaves facility executives with different rules in different states," *Building Operating Management* (October 1999), p. 51.

25. Alfred North Whitehead, *Science and the Modern World* (New York: Mentor, 1964), p. 58.

26. Harry Howe Ranson, *Central Intelligence and National Security* (Cambridge, Mass.: Harvard University Press, 1958), p. 214.

27. *Ibid.*

28. Huston Smith, "The Death and Rebirth of Metaphysics," *Process & Divinity*, ed. William L. Reese and Eugene Freeman (LaSalle, Ill: Open Court Publishing Co., 1964), p. 46.

29. Richard Wilk, "When Theory Is Everything, Scholarship Suffers," *The Chronicle of Higher Education*, 45:44 (9 July 1999), p. A52.

30. *Ibid.*

31. Kenneth E. Boulding, *The Image* (Ann Arbor, Mich.: The University of Michigan Press, 1956), p. 10.

FIVE: Rehumanizing Disciplinarity

1. Henry Winthrop, "Generalists and Specialists," *The Journal of Higher Education,* 37:4 (April 1966), p. 200.

2. Paul Dressel, "Liberal Education: Developing the Characteristics of the Liberally Educated Person," *Liberal Education* (Fall 1979), p. 320.

3. *Ibid.*, p. 317.

4. Russell L. Ackoff, "Systems, Organizations, and Interdisciplinary Research," *Yearbook of the Society for General Systems Theory*, vol. 5. p. 6.

5. Paul Dressel, "Liberal Education: Developing the Characteristics of the Liberally Educated Person," p. 322.

6. Alfred North Whitehead, *The Aims of Education* (New York: Mentor, 1964), p. 18.

7. Henry Winthrop, "Generalists and Specialists," p. 200.

8. Jamie Chamberlin, "Devine Encourages Psychologists to Expand Their Vision," *Monitor,* 31:1 (January 2000) p. 80.

9. Robin Wilson, "The Remaking of Math," *The Chronicle of Higher Education*. 46:18 (7 January 2000), p. A16.

10. George Waltz, "Thinking Ahead with Vannevar Bush," *International Science and Technology,* Prototype Issue (January 1961), p.62.

11. Earl J. McGrath, "The Time Bomb of Technocratic Education" *Change* (September 1974), p. 24.

12. Albert Einstein, *Out of My Later Years* (New York: The Philosophical Library, Inc., 1950). p. 50.

13. *Ibid.*

14. Peter Drucker, "The Coming Changes in Our School Systems," *The Wall Street Journal*, 197:42 (3 March 1981), p. 30.

15. Stuart Chase, "Are You and Generalist or Specialist?," *Introduction to College Life*, ed. Norman T. Bell, Richard W. Burckhardt, Richard B. Lawhead (New York: Houghton-Mifflin, 1966), p. 49.

16. Ram Charan and Geoffrey Colvin, "Why CEOs Fail," *Fortune*, 139:12 (21 June 1999) p. 78.

17. Betsey Morris and Patricia Seller, "What Really Happened at Coke," *Fortune*, 141:1 (10 January 2000), p. 115.

18. *Ibid.*

19. Susan M. Rakley, "When I Stopped Yelling, Everybody Started Listening," *Medical Economics*. 76:19 (11 October 1999), p. 131.

20. Martin Buber, *I and Thou* (New York: Charles Scribner's Sons, 1970), p. 51.

21. Madeleine Jacobs, "Experiment—And You'll See," *Chemical & Engineering News*, 77:46 (13 November 1999), p. 3.

22. Henry Winthrop, "The Institute of Intellectual Synthesis," *The Educational Forum*, 30:2 (January 1996), p. 223.

23. Gerald Graff, "Colleges Are Depriving Students of a Connected View of Scholarship," *The Chronicle of Higher Education*, 37:22 (15 February 1991). p. A48.

24. Alfred North Whitehead, *The Aims of Education*, p. 18.

25. *Ibid.*

26. Henry Winthrop, "The Institute of Intellectual Synthesis," p. 225.

27. Ackoff, "Systems, Organizations, and Interdisciplinary Research," p. 6.

28. Herbert W. Richardson, "A Philosophy of Unity," *The Harvard Theological Review*, 80:1 (January 1967), p. 2.

29. Kenneth E. Boulding, *The Image* (Ann Arbor, Mich.: University of Michigan Press, 1968), p. 163.

30. Norbert Weiner, *Cybernetics* (Cambridge, Mass.: The MIT Press, 1961), p. 19.

31. Martin J. Cannon, *Management* (Boston: Little, Brown and Company, 1977), p. 141.

32. Whitehead, *The Aims of Education*, p. 22.

33. Alfred North Whitehead, *Science and The Modern World* (New York: Mentor, 1964), p. 58.

34. Alfred North Whitehead, *Science and the Modern World*, p. vii.

35. John Dewey, "The Relation of Science and Philosophy as the Basis of Education," *School and Society*, 47:1215 (9 April 1938), p.20.

36. Robert Maynard Hutchins, *The Conflict of Education in a Democratic Society* (New York: Harper & Row, Publishers, 1953), p. 76.

37. *THIS IS MIT: MASSACHUSETTS INSTITUTE OF TECHNOLOGY CATALOGUE*, 1961-1962 BULLETIN p. 6

38. Fred Davis, "The Cabdriver and His Fare," *The Social Dimensions of Work* (ed.) Clifton D. Bryant (Englewood Cliffs, N.J.: Prentice-Hall; 1972), p. 408.

39. *Ibid.*

40. Jerome B. Weisner, *The Challenge of Technology* (New York: The Conference Board; 1966), p. 5.

41. Melissa Wahl and Susan Chandler, "Jobless Rate Still Sliding," *Chicago Tribune* (5 February 2000), p. 1.

42. Janet Kidd Stewart, "Drop in Jobs Boosts Hope Fed's Work May Be Done," *Chicago Tribune*, (5 August 2001), p. 1.

43. "The Speech," *The Chicago Tribune* (28 January 2000), p. 9.

44. Wilbur J. Cohen, "Education and Learning," *The Annals of the American Academy of Political and Social Sciences*, Philadelphia. vol. 373 (September 1967), p. 82.

45. Philip W. Semas, "U.S. Universities Don't Know What They Are Doing or Why, Robert M. Hutchins Says," *The Chronicle of Higher Education*, 4:22 (9 March 1970), p. 5.

SIX: Dehumanizing Disciplinary Motions

1. Alfred North Whitehead, *Science and the Modern World* (New York: Mentor, 1964), p. vii.

2. *THIS IS MIT: MASSACHUSETTS INSTITUTE OF TECHNOLOGY CATALOGUE, 1961-1962 BULLETIN* (Cambridge, Mass.: Massachusetts Institute of Technology), p. 6.

3. Fred Davis, "The Cabdriver and His Fare," in *The Social Dimensions of Work*, ed. Clifton D. Bryant (Englewood Cliffs, N.J.: Prentice-Hall, 1972), p. 408.

4. *Ibid.*

5. William B. Scott/Kirtland AFB, N.M., "Special Ops Students Train to 'Own the

Night," *Aviation Weekly & Space Technology* (26 January 1998), p. 55.

6. Michael J. Walsh, Lt. Cmdr., USN (Ret.), *SEAL* (New York: Simon & Schuster, 1995), p. 287.

7. *Ibid.*

8. Roy Boehm, *First SEAL* (New York: Simon & Schuster, 1997), inside back cover.

9. *THIS IS M.I.T. 1961-1962*, p. 43.

10. Ripley Hotch, "The Accidental CEO," *Communication News*, 36:12. (Decenber 1999), p. 15.

11. Russell V. Gerbman, "Corporate Universities 101," *HR Magazine*, 45:2 (February 2000), p. 201.

12. James Carney, "The Bodyguards: Shadows and Shields," *Time*, 152:4 (27 July 1998), p. 23.

13. John Flynn Rooney, "Continuing Education Classes Urged for Judges," *Chicago Daily Law Bulletin*, 143:209 (24 October 1997), p. 1.

14. Chief Judge Marvin E. Aspen, "Jurors are Community Heroes," *The Chicago Tribune* Thursday, (3 June 1999), p. 22. Section 1.

15. Leo Ciaramiaro, "Sciullo Looks at Legal Education," *Juris: School of Law, Duquesne University* (Fall 1997), p. 8.

16. David Pilling, "The Future of Medicine," *Financial Times* (31 December 1999), p. 10.

17. Alfred North Whitehead, *The Aimes of Education* (New York: Mentor, 1964), p. xl.

18. Whitehead, *Science and the Modern World*, p. 54.

SEVEN: Rehumanizing Data

1. Alfred North Whitehead, *The Aims of Education* (New York: Mentor, 1964), p. 23.

2. *Ibid.*, p. 36.

3. *Ibid.*, p. 37.

4. *Ibid.*, p. 18.

5. *Ibid.*, p. 97.

6. *Ibid.*, p. 116.

7. Karl Popper, *Conjectures and Refutations* (London: Routledge & Keegan Paul, Ltd., 1969), p. 46.

8. Vincent Kiernan, "Sophisticated Software Is Reshaping the Way Scientists Use Statistics," *The Chronicle of Higher Education*, 45:1 (8 January 1999), p. A26.

9. Jeremy Campbell, *The Improbable Machine* (New York: Simon & Schuster, 1989), p. 128.

10. John Mesenbrink, "Sky Spy," *Security*, 36:12 (December 1999), p. 14.

11. John Douglas, *Mind Hunter* (New York: Simon & Schuster, 1995), p. 82.

12. Sandra Sobieraj, "Democrats Debate Profiling," *Chicago Sun-Times*, (22 February 2000), p. 14.

13. *THIS IS MIT: MASSACHUSETTS INSTITUTE OF TECHNOLOGY CATALOGUE, 1961-1962 BULLETIN*, p. 46.

14. Whitehead, *The Aims of Education*, p. 94.

15. Huston C. Smith, "The Death and Rebirth of Metaphysics," *Process and Divinity*, ed. William L. Reese and Eugene Freeman (LaSalle, Ill.: Open Court, 1964), p. 40.

16. John Clarke, "Homer and Aristotle," *Liberal Education* (Fall 1979), p. 398.

17. Whitehead, *The Aims of Education*, p. xl.

18. *THIS IS MIT: MASSACHUSETTS INSTITUTE OF TECHNOLOGY CATALOGUE, 1961-1962 BULLETIN*, p. 43.

19. Richard Wilk, "When Theory Is Everything, Scholarship Suffers," *The Chronicle of Higher Education*, 45:20 (9 July 1999), p. A52.

BIBLIOGRAPHY

Ackoff, Russell L. "Systems, Organizations, and Interdisciplinary Research," *Yearbook of the Society for General System Theory.* Volume 6, 1961.

Aspen, Marvin E. "Jurors Are Community Heroes," *The Chicago Tribune.* 3 June 1999.

Bellman, Richard E. "Dynamic Programming, Intelligent Machines, and Self-Organizing Systems," *Symposium on the Mathematical Theory of Automata, Polytechnic Institute of Brooklyn,* 24, 25, 26 April 1962.

Bevington, David. ed. *The Complete Works of William Shakespeare.* New York: Longman, 1997.

Blondin, George and David Green. "A Unifying Model of Bioenergetics," *Chemical & Engineering News.* 53:20, 10 November 1975.

Boehm, Roy. *First SEAL.* New York: Simon & Schuster, 1997.

Boulding, Kenneth E. *The Image.* Ann Arbor, Mich.: University of Michigan Press, 1956.

Bowles, Mark Donald. *Crisis in the Information Age?* Ann Arbor, Mich.: University Microfilms, Inc., 1999.

Boyer, Ernest L. "Changing Dimensions in Higher Education," *The College Board Review.* No. 87, Spring 1973.

Brown, Roger. "From Codability to Coding Ability," *Learning About Learning,* ed. Jerome S. Bruner Washington: U. S. Government Printing Office, 1966.

Buber, Martin. *I and Thou.* New York: Charles Scribner, 1970.

Campbell, Jeremy. *The Improbable Machine.* New York: Simon & Schuster, 1989.

Cannon, Martin J. *Management.* Boston: Little, Brown, and Company, 1977.

Carney, James. "The Bodyguards: Shadows and Shields," *Time.* 152:4

Chamberlin, Jamie. "Devine Encourages Psychologists to Expand Their Vision," *Monitor.* 31:1, January 2000.

Charan, Ram and Geoffrey Colvin. "Why CEOs Fail," *Fortune.* 139:12, 21 June 1999.

Chase, Stuart. "Are You a Generalist or Specialist?," *Introduction to College Life,* ed.

Norman T. Bell, Richard W. Burckhardt, Richard B. Lawhead. New York: Houghton-Mifflin, 1966.

Ciaramiaro, Leo. "Sciullo Looks at Legal Education," *Juris: School of Law, Duquesne University*, Fall 1997.

Clarke, John. "Homer and Aristotle," *Liberal Education*, Fall 1979.

Clynes, Manfred. "Toward a View of Man," *Biomedical Engineering Systems* ed. Manfred Clynes and J. N. Milsum, New York: McGraw-Hill, 1970.

Cohen, Wilber J. "Education and Learning," *The Annals of the American Academy of Political and Social Sciences*. Philadelphia, vol. 373, September 1967.

Davis, Fred. "The Cabdriver and His Fare," *The Social Dimensions of Work*, ed. Clifton D. Bryant, Englewood Cliffs, N.J.: Prentice-Hall, 1972.

Dewey, John. "The Relation of Science and Philosophy as the Basis of Education," *School and Society*, 47:1215 19 April 1938.

Doherty, James J. "A Few Suggestions for Handling Criminal Appeals," *Case & Comment*, 75:1 January-February, 1970.

Douglas, John. *Mind Hunter*. New York: Simon & Schuster, 1995.

Dressel, Paul. "Liberal Education: Developing the Characteristics of the Liberally Educated Person," *Liberal Education*, Fall 1979.

Drucker, Peter. "The Coming Changes in Our School Systems," *The Wall Street Journal*, 197:42 3 March 1981.

Einstein, Albert. *Out of My Later Years*. New York: The Philosophical Library, Inc. 1950.

Eliade, Mircea. *Myth and Reality*. New York: Harper Torchbooks, 1963.

Fabos, Bettina and Michelle D. Young "Telecommunication in the Classroom," *Review of Educational Research*, 69:3, Fall 1999.

Fiske, Edward B. "Booming Corporate Education Rivals College Programs, Study Says," *The New York Times*. 34:46, 26 January 1985.

Freire, Paulo. *Pedagogy of the Oppressed*, trans. Myra Bergman Ramos, New York: Continuum, 1992.

Gardner, John W. "Agenda for the Colleges and Universities," *Campus 1980*. ed. Alvin C. Eurich, New York: Dell Publishing Company, Inc., 1968.

Gertman, Russell V. "Corporate Universities 101" *HR Magazine*, 45:2, February 2000.

Graff, Gerald. "Colleges Are Depriving Students of a Connected View of Scholarship," *The Chronicle of Higher Education*, 37:22, 15 February 1991.

Hall, Jerome. "Perennial Problems in Criminal Law," *The Hofstra Law Review*, 1:1 Spring 1973.

Hotch, Ripley. "The Accidental CEO," *Communication News*, 33:12, December 1999.

Hutchins, Robert Maynard. *The Conflict of Education in Democratic Society.* New York: Harper & Row, 1953.

————————. *The Learning Society.* New York: Mentor, 1966.

Jacobs, Madeleine. "Experiment—And You'll See," *Chemical & Engineering News*, 77:46, 13 November 1999.

Johnson, Richard A., Kast, Fremont E. and James A. Rosenzweig. *The Theory and Management of Systems.* 3rd edition, New York: McGraw-Hill Book Company, 1973.

Jones, R. L. "Beyond School Walls," *Action in Teacher Education,* 4:4, Fall 1982.

Kazanjian, Michael M. *"Theology of Culture: Some Aspects of the Sacred Dimensions of the Secular." Delta Epsilon Sigma Bulletin,* 16:1, March 1971.

Kiernan, Vincent. "Sophisticated Software is Reshaping the Way Scientists Use Statistics," *The Chronicle of Higher Education,* 45:1, 8 January 1999.

Liveright, A. A. "Learning Never Ends: A Plan for Continuing Education," *Campus 1980.* ed. Alvin C. Eurich, New York: Dell Publishing Company, 1968.

Lobash, Michael. "Two Codes, Too Bad: A Failed Attempt to Create a National Fire Code Leaves Facility Executives with Different Rules in Different States, *Building Operating Management,* October 1999.

Lutrin, Carl E. and Allen K. Settle. *American Public Administration: Concepts and Cases.* 2nd edition, San Luis Opispo, Cal.: Mayfield Publishing Company, 1976.

McGrath, Earl J. "The Time Bomb of Technocratic Education," *Change,* September 1974.

Mesenbrink, John. "Sky Spy," *Security,* 36:12, December 1999.

Morris, Betsey and Patricia Seller. "What Really Happened at Coke?," *Fortune,* 141:1, 10 January 2000.

Neubauer, David W. *America's Courts and the Criminal Justice System,* 5th edition Belmont, Cal.: Wadsworth Publishing Company. 1996.

Perrin, Norman. *Jesus and the Language of the Kingdom.* Philadelphia: Fortress Press, 1976.

Pilling, David. "The Future of Medicine," *Financial Times,* 31 December 1999.

Pitt-Rivers, Julian. *The Fate of Shechem, or the Politics of Sex.* London: Cambridge University Press. 1977.

Popper, Karl. *Conjectures and Refutations.* London: Routledge & Kegan Paul, Ltd. 1969.

Rabasca, Lisa. "Mischel Sees Psychological Review as Forum to Connect with New Fields," *Monitor,* 31:1, January 2000.

Rakley, Susan M. "When I stopped Yelling, Everybody Started Listening," *Medical Economics,* 76:19, 11 October 1999.

Ransom, Harry Howe. *Central Intelligence and National Security.* Cambridge, Mass: Harvard University Press. 1958.

Richardson, Herbert W. "A Philosophy of Unity," *The Harvard Theological Review,* 80:1, January 1967.

Rodin, Mariam, Karen Michaelson and Gerald M. Britan. "Systems Theory in Anthropology," *Current Anthropology,* 10:4, December 1978.

Rossi, Rosalind. "Daley Invites Parents to First Day of School," *Chicago Sun-Times,* 19 August 2000.

Scott, William B. "Special Ops Students Train to 'Own the Night,'" *Aviation Weekly & Space Technology,* 26 January 1998.

Semas, Philip W. "U. S. Universities Don't Know What They Are Doing or Why, Robert M. Hutchins Says," *The Chronicle of Higher Education,* 4:22, 9 March 1970.

Smith, Huston C. "The Death and Rebirth of Metaphysics," *Process & Divinity.* ed. William L. Reese and Eugene Freeman, LaSalle, Ill.: Open Court Publishing Co., 1964.

Sobiaraj, Sandra. "Democrats Debate Profiling," *Chicago Sun-Times,* 22 February 2000.

THIS IS MIT: MASSACHUSETTS INSTITUTE OF TECHNOLOGY CATALOGUE, 1961-1962 BULLETIN.

Thomas, Martha W. "Business Communication in the Modern Age," *Business & Eco-*

nomic Review. 44:4, July-August-September 1998.

Wahl, Melissa and Susan Chandler. "Jobless Rate Still Sliding," *The Chicago Tribune,* 15 February 2000.

Walsh, Michael J. Lt. Cmdr., USN (Ret.), *SEAL.* New York: Simon & Schuster, 1995.

Waltz, George. "Thinking Ahead with Vannevar Bush," *International Science and Technology.* Prototype Issue, January 1961.

Warren, Robert. "The Speech," *The Chicago Tribune.* 28 January 2000.

Webster's Third World International Dictionary. Springfield, Mass.: Merriam-Webster, 1993, p.108.

Whitehead, Alfred North. *Science and the Modern World.* New York: Mentor, 1964.

_____. *The Aims of Education.* New York: Mentor, 1964.

Wiener, Norbert. *Cybernetics.* Cambridge, Mass.: The MIT Press, 1961.

Wiesner, Jerome B. *The Challenge of Technology.* New York: The Conference Board, 1966.

Wilk, Richard. "When Theory Is Everything, Scholarship Suffers," *The Chronicle of Higher Education.* 45:44, 9 July 1999.

Wilson, Robin. "The Remaking of Math," *The Chronicle of Higher Education,* 46:18, 7 January 2000.

Winthrop, Henry. "Generalists and Specialists," *The Journal of Higher Education,* 37:4, April 1966.

_____. "The Institute for Intellectual Synthesis," *The Educational Forum,* 30:2, January 1966.

Wittgenstein, Ludwig. *Philosophical Investigations.* New York: Macmillan, 1958.

_____. *Tractatus Logico-Philosophicus.* London: Routlege & Kegan Paul, 1961.

Yamada, Reiko. "Higher Education Reform: Toward a Lifelong Learning Society," *CAEL Forum and News.* 23:1, Fall 1999.

ABOUT THE AUTHOR

Michael Kazanjian is with the Publications Group of DePaul University, Chicago. The present volume is his second book. His first book is *Phenomenology and Education: Cosmology, Co-Being, and Core Curriculum* (Rodopi, 1998). Kazanjian has authored or coauthored twenty scholars papers and numerous conference presentations. He contributed to the Bernard J. Boelen *Festschrift* at DePaul University and the Paul Sebestyen *Festschrift* at North Park University. Kazanjian's papers have appeared in *U.S. House Hearings, Delta Epsilon Sigma Bulletin, Contemporary Philosophy, The Meaning of Life*, and the *Newsletter of the Association for Process Philosophy of Education*. He is past-president of the University of Chicago/DePaul University Chapter of Phi Delta Kappa, the Professional Education Fraternity. He is a member of the Association for Process Philosophy of Education, American Philosophical Association, Society for Phenomenology and Existential Philosophy, Association for the Development of Philosophy Teaching, Philosophy of Education Society, Environmental and Architectural Phenomenology, and the Association for Professional and Practical Ethics. He has taught philosophy of education at DePaul University and North Park University. At Waubonsee Community College, he taught philosophy, and developed an interactive distance learning course on the philosophy of work.

INDEX

State University of New York (SUNY) at
    Stony Brook 15

Temple Sinai 21
The Image 55, 66
Theory and Management of Systems 18
Thomas, Martha W. 30
Thou 25, 26
Three Mile Island 97, 98
Tractatus Logico-Philosophicus 18

value-free 4, 7, 30, 72, 96

Walsh, Michael J. 81
Wayne State University College of
    Lifelong Learning 15
Weiner, Norbert 18, 67
West Point 60
Whitehead, Albert North 2, 3, 9, 10, 11,
    13, 25, 26, 27, 40, 41, 43, 51, 60, 65,
    66, 67, 69, 70, 89, 91, 92, 96, 97
wholeness 1, 2, 4, 5, 7, 11, 18, 20, 23, 29,
    33, 44, 45, 48, 55, 58, 61, 63, 64, 65,
    66, 68, 72, 98, 99, 105
Winthrop, Henry 8, 57, 60, 65, 66
Wittgenstein, Ludwig 18, 19

VIBS

The **Value Inquiry Book Series** is co-sponsored by:

Adler School of Professional Psychology
American Indian Philosophy Association
American Maritain Association
American Society for Value Inquiry
Association for Process Philosophy of Education
Canadian Society for Philosophical Practice
Center for Bioethics, University of Turku
Center for Professional and Applied Ethics, University of North Carolina at Charlotte
Center for Research in Cognitive Science, Autonomous University of Barcelona
Centre for Applied Ethics, Hong Kong Baptist University
Centre for Cultural Research, Aarhus University
Centre for Professional Ethics, University of Central Lancashire
Centre for the Study of Philosophy and Religion, University College of Cape Breton
College of Education and Allied Professions, Bowling Green State University
College of Liberal Arts, Rochester Institute of Technology
Concerned Philosophers for Peace
Conference of Philosophical Societies
Department of Moral and Social Philosophy, University of Helsinki
Gannon University
Gilson Society
Ikeda University
Institute of Philosophy of the High Council of Scientific Research, Spain
International Academy of Philosophy of the Principality of Liechtenstein
International Center for the Arts, Humanities, and Value Inquiry
International Society for Universal Dialogue
Natural Law Society
Personalist Discussion Group
Philosophical Society of Finland
Philosophy Born of Struggle Association
Philosophy Seminar, University of Mainz
Pragmatism Archive
R.S. Hartman Institute for Formal and Applied Axiology
Research Institute, Lakeridge Health Corporation
Russian Philosophical Society
Society for Iberian and Latin-American Thought
Society for the Philosophic Study of Genocide and the Holocaust
Society for the Philosophy of Sex and Love
Yves R. Simon Institute

Titles Published

Mill's Notorious Proof. A volume in **Universal Justice**

19.   Michael H. Mitias, Editor, *Philosophy and Architecture.*

20.   Roger T. Simonds, *Rational Individualism: The Perennial Philosophy of Legal Interpretation.* A volume in **Natural Law Studies**

21.   William Pencak, *The Conflict of Law and Justice in the Icelandic Sagas*

22.   Samuel M. Natale and Brian M. Rothschild, Editors, *Values, Work, Education: The Meanings of Work*

23.   N. Georgopoulos and Michael Heim, Editors, *Being Human in the Ultimate: Studies in the Thought of John M. Anderson*

24.   Robert Wesson and Patricia A. Williams, Editors, *Evolution and Human Values*

25.   Wim J. van der Steen, *Facts, Values, and Methodology: A New Approach to Ethics*

26.   Avi Sagi and Daniel Statman, *Religion and Morality*

27.   Albert William Levi, *The High Road of Humanity: The Seven Ethical Ages of Western Man*, Edited by Donald Phillip Verene and Molly Black Verene

28.   Samuel M. Natale and Brian M. Rothschild, Editors, *Work Values: Education, Organization, and Religious Concerns*

29.   Laurence F. Bove and Laura Duhan Kaplan, Editors, *From the Eye of the Storm: Regional Conflicts and the Philosophy of Peace.* A volume in **Philosophy of Peace**

30.   Robin Attfield, *Value, Obligation, and Meta-Ethics*

31.   William Gerber, *The Deepest Questions You Can Ask About God: As Answered by the World's Great Thinkers*

32.   Daniel Statman, *Moral Dilemmas*

33.   Rem B. Edwards, Editor, *Formal Axiology and Its Critics.* A volume in **Hartman Institute Axiology Studies**

34.   George David Miller and Conrad P. Pritscher, *On Education and Values: In Praise of Pariahs and Nomads.* A volume in **Philosophy of Education**

35.   Paul S. Penner, *Altruistic Behavior: An Inquiry into Motivation*

K. Skrupskelis

67. Lansana Keita, *The Human Project and the Temptations of Science*

68. Michael M. Kazanjian, *Phenomenology and Education: Cosmology, Co-Being, and Core Curriculum*. A volume in **Philosophy of Education**

69. James W. Vice, *The Reopening of the American Mind: On Skepticism and Constitutionalism*

70. Sarah Bishop Merrill, *Defining Personhood: Toward the Ethics of Quality in Clinical Care*

71. Dane R. Gordon, *Philosophy and Vision*

72. Alan Milchman and Alan Rosenberg, Editors, *Postmodernism and the Holocaust*. A volume in **Holocaust and Genocide Studies**

73. Peter A. Redpath, *Masquerade of the Dream Walkers: Prophetic Theology from the Cartesians to Hegel*. A volume in **Studies in the History of Western Philosophy**

74. Malcolm D. Evans, *Whitehead and Philosophy of Education: The Seamless Coat of Learning*. A volume in **Philosophy of Education**

75. Warren E. Steinkraus, *Taking Religious Claims Seriously: A Philosophy of Religion*, edited by Michael H. Mitias. A volume in **Universal Justice**

76. Thomas Magnell, Editor, *Values and Education*

77. Kenneth A. Bryson, *Persons and Immortality*. A volume in **Natural Law Studies**

78. Steven V. Hicks, *International Law and the Possibility of a Just World Order: An Essay on Hegel's Universalism*. A volume in **Universal Justice**

79. E. F. Kaelin, *Texts on Texts and Textuality: A Phenomenology of Literary Art*, Edited by Ellen J. Burns

80. Amihud Gilead, Saving Possibilities: A Study in Philosophical Psychology. *A volume in Philosophy and Psychology*

81. André Mineau, *The Making of the Holocaust: Ideology and Ethics in the Systems Perspective*. A volume in **Holocaust and Genocide Studies**

82. Howard P. Kainz, *Politically Incorrect Dialogues: Topics Not Discussed in*

83.   Veikko Launis, Juhani Pietarinen, and Juha Räikkä, Editors, *Genes and Morality: New Essays*. A volume in **Nordic Value Studies**

84.   Steven Schroeder, *The Metaphysics of Cooperation: A Study of F. D. Maurice*

85.   Caroline Joan ("Kay") S. Picart, *Thomas Mann and Friedrich Nietzsche: Eroticism, Death, Music, and Laughter*. A volume in **Central-European Value Studies**

86.   G. John M. Abbarno, Editor, *The Ethics of Homelessness: Philosophical Perspectives*

87.   James Giles, Editor, *French Existentialism: Consciousness, Ethics, and Relations with Others*. A volume in **Nordic Value Studies**

88.   Deane Curtin and Robert Litke, Editors, *Institutional Violence*. A volume in **Philosophy of Peace**

89.   Yuval Lurie, *Cultural Beings: Reading the Philosophers of Genesis*

90.   Sandra A. Wawrytko, Editor, *The Problem of Evil: An Intercultural Exploration*. A volume in **Philosophy and Psychology**

91.   Gary J. Acquaviva, *Values, Violence, and Our Future*. A volume in **Hartman Institute Axiology Studies**

92.   Michael R. Rhodes, *Coercion: A Nonevaluative Approach*

93.   Jacques Kriel, *Matter, Mind, and Medicine: Transforming the Clinical Method*

94.   Haim Gordon, *Dwelling Poetically: Educational Challenges in Heidegger's Thinking on Poetry*. A volume in **Philosophy of Education**

95.   Ludwig Grünberg, *The Mystery of Values: Studies in Axiology*, edited by Cornelia Grünberg and Laura Grünberg

96.   Gerhold K. Becker, Editor, *The Moral Status of Persons: Perspectives on Bioethics*. A volume in **Studies in Applied Ethics**

97.   Roxanne Claire Farrar, *Sartrean Dialectics: A Method for Critical Discourse on Aesthetic Experience*

98.   Ugo Spirito, *Memoirs of the Twentieth Century*. Translated from Italian

and edited by Anthony G. Costantini. A volume in **Values in Italian Philosophy**

99.   Steven Schroeder, *Between Freedom and Necessity: An Essay on the Place of Value*

100.   Foster N. Walker, *Enjoyment and the Activity of Mind: Dialogues on Whitehead and Education*. A volume in **Philosophy of Education**

101.   Avi Sagi, Kierkegaard, *Religion, and Existence: The Voyage of the Self.* Translated from Hebrew by Batya Stein

102.   Bennie R. Crockett, Jr., Editor, *Addresses of the Mississippi Philosophical Associati* A volume in **Histories and Addresses of Philosophical Societies**

103.   Paul van Dijk, *Anthropology in the Age of Technology: The Philosophical Contribution of Günther Anders*

104.   Giambattista Vico, *Universal Right.* Translated from Latin and Edited by Giorgio Pinton and Margaret Diehl. A volume in **Values in Italian Philosophy**

105.   Judith Presler and Sally J. Scholz, Editors, *Peacemaking: Lessons from the Past, Visions for the Future*. A volume in **Philosophy of Peace**

106.   Dennis Bonnette, *Origin of the Human Species*. A volume in **Studies in the History of Western Philosophy**

107.   Phyllis Chiasson, *Peirce's Pragmatism: The Design for Thinking.* A volume in **Studies in Pragmatism and Values**

108.   Dan Stone, Editor, *Theoretical Interpretations of the Hol*ocaust. A volume in **Holocaust and Genocide Studies**

109.   Raymond Angelo Belliotti, *What Is the Meaning of Human Life?*
110.   Lennart Nordenfelt, *Health, Science, and Ordinary Language*, with Contributions by George Khushf and K. W. M. Fulford

111.   Daryl Koehn, *Local Insights, Global Ethics for Business*. A volume in **Studies in Applied Ethics**

112.   Matti Häyry and Tuija Takala, Editors, *The Future of Value Inquiry.* A volume in **Nordic Value Studies**

113.   Conrad P. Pritscher, *Quantum Learning: Beyond Duality*

114.   Thomas M. Dicken and Rem B. Edwards, *Dialogues on Values and Centers*

of Value: Old Friends, New Thoughts. A volume in **Hartman Institute Axiology Studies**

115.   Rem B. Edwards, *What Caused the Big Bang?* A volume in **Philosophy and Religion**

116.   Jon Mills, Editor, *A Pedagogy of Becoming.* A volume in **Philosophy of Education**

117.   Robert T. Radford, *Cicero: A Study in the Origins of Republican Philosophy.* A volume in **Studies in the History of Western Philosophy**

118.   Arleen L. F. Salles and María Julia Bertomeu, Editors, *Bioethics: Latin American Perspectives.* A volume in **Philosophy in Latin America**

119.   Nicola Abbagnano, *The Human Project: The Year 2000*, with an Interview by Guiseppe Grieco. Translated from Italian by Bruno Martini and Nino Langiulli. Edited with an introduction by Nino Langiulli. A volume in **Studies in the History of Western Philosophy**

120.   Daniel M. Haybron, Editor, *Earth's Abominations: Philosophical Studies of Evil.* A volume in **Personalist Studies**

121.   Anna T. Challenger, *Philosophy and Art in Gurdjieff's Beelzebub: A Modern Sufi Odyssey*

122.   George David Miller, *Peace, Value, and Wisdom: The Educational Philosophy of Daisaku Ikeda.* A volume in **Daisaku Ikeda Studies**

123.   Haim Gordon and Rivca Gordon, *Sophistry and Twentieth-Century Art*

124.   Thomas O Buford and Harold H. Oliver, Editors *Personalism Revisited: Its Proponents and Critics.* A volume in **Histories and Addresses of Philosophical Societies**
125.   Avi Sagi, *Albert Camus and the Philosophy of the Absurd.* Translated from Hebrew by Batya Stein

126.   Robert S. Hartman, *The Knowledge of Good: Critique of Axiologic l Reason.* Expanded translation from the Spanish by Robert S. Hartman. Edited by Arthur R. Ellis and Rem B. Edwards. A volume in **Hartman Institute Axiology Studies**

127.   Alison Bailey and Paula J. Smithka, Editors. *Community, Diversity, and Difference: Implications for Peace.* A volume in **Philosophy of Peace**